Map Key

M000222881

Other Books of Interest

60 Hikes within 60 Miles Boston

60 Hikes within 60 Miles New York City

The Appalachian Trail Hiker

The Best in Tent Camping New England

The Best in Tent Camping New York State

GPS Outdoors

Hikers' and Backpackers' Guide for Treating Medical Emergencies

MOUNTAINS for MORTALS

SCENIC SUMMITS FOR HIKERS

NEW ENGLAND

Ron and Nancy Chase

MENASHA RIDGE PRESS
Birmingham, Alabama

DISCLAIMER

This book is meant only as a guide to select trails in the vicinity of New England and does not guarantee hiker safety in any way—you hike at your own risk. Neither Menasha Ridge Press nor Ron and Nancy Chase is liable for property loss or damage, personal injury, or death that result in any way from accessing or hiking the trails described in the following pages. Please be aware that hikers have been injured in the area. Be especially cautious when walking on or near boulders, steep inclines, and drop-offs, and do not attempt to explore terrain that may be beyond your abilities. To help ensure an uneventful hike, please read carefully the introduction to this book, and perhaps get further safety information and guidance from other sources. Familiarize yourself thoroughly with the areas you intend to visit before venturing out. Ask questions, and prepare for the unforeseen. Familiarize yourself with current weather reports, maps of the area you intend to visit, and any relevant park regulations.

Copyright © 2008 Ron and Nancy Chase
All rights reserved.
Manufactured in the United States of America
Published by Menasha Ridge Press
First edition, first printing, 2008

Library of Congress Cataloging-in-Publication Data

Chase, Ron, 1947–

Mountains for mortals : New England : scenic peaks for hikers and backpackers / by Ron and Nancy Chase.—1st ed.

　　p. cm.

Includes index.

ISBN-13: 978-0-89732-621-6

ISBN-10: 0-89732-621-0

1. Hiking—New England—Guidebooks. 2. Mountains—New England—Guidebooks. 3. Trails—New England—Guidebooks. 4. New England—Guidebooks. I. Chase, Nancy. II. Title.

GV199.42.N38C43 2008

917.4044—dc22

　　　　　　　2008011680

Cover design by Travis Bryant

Text design by Annie Long

Cover photo by Ron Chase

All other photos by Nancy and Ron Chase

Maps and elevation profiles drawn by Nancy Chase and Scott McGrew

Menasha Ridge Press
P.O. Box 43673
Birmingham, AL 35243
www.menasharidge.com

To our parents, Anna Bennett Chase, Ralph A. Chase Jr., and Christine Berry Gilman.

table *of* contents

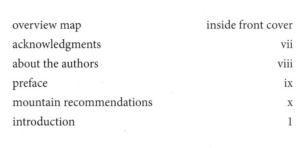

acknowledgments

This book would not have been possible without our many hiking companions. For us, the shared camaraderie is perhaps the foremost aspect of the hiking experience. We began our mountaineering adventures more than 30 years ago with our sons, Eric and Adam, when they were small children. During the early years, friends John and Diane Stokinger were regular hiking partners. The orienteering skills that John shared with us were of invaluable benefit. About 15 years ago, we endeavored to climb the 100 highest peaks in New England with a group of friends. This challenge provided us with the incentive and the opportunity to explore the great New England peaks. Frequent mountain accomplices were Richard Bedard, Randy Berube, Dave Boyle, John Brower, Tee Brower, Lloyd Brown, Diane Chase, Jayne Chase, Gary Cole, Suzanne Cole, Alice Douglas, Dave Duggan, Brent Elwell, Brad Fox, Ken Gordon, Susan Gordon, Ed Hawkins, Joline Hendershot, Tom Homsted, Audrey Ingersoll, Sam Jamke, Bill "Grampy" Kaiser, Ted Kaler, Bill Laidley, Pierre Larue, Josee LeCulyer, Sonny Martineau, Tom Meredith, Mike Moody, Patricia Moody, Laura Neal, Josee Paquet, Greg Pelotte, Sharon Pelotte, Taylor Pelotte, Amanda Shorette, Andrea Reed, Rodney Reed, Daryn Slover, Gretchen Slover, Terry Tzavarrus, Robin Wade, Dave Wallace, Steve Ward, Bob White, Kris White, Lori White, Laurie Wunder, Carolyn Young, Frank Yulling, and many, many more. Dave Boyle, Suzanne Cole, Ken Gordon, Pete Levesque, and John Stokinger made meaningful contributions to this book.

Copy editor Holly Cross was especially professional, supportive, and helpful. Without the early encouragement and guidance provided by Russell Helms, this book would not have become a reality.

about *the* authors

Maine natives Ron and Nancy Chase currently reside in Topsham, Maine, and have two grown sons. They have hiked extensively in New England for more than 30 years and shared treks and mountaineering adventures throughout the United States, eastern Canada, Scotland, France, Switzerland, and Costa Rica. Both have an abiding love of the outdoors. When not hiking in the mountains, they enjoy kayaking, canoeing, cycling, and skiing. Together, they operate a tax-consulting business.

Nancy, formerly Treasurer of the Maine Chapter of the Appalachian Mountain Club (AMC), is currently active in the Penobscot Paddle and Chowder Society (PPCS). In 2000, the AMC Four Thousand Footer Committee awarded her a certificate for completing the 100 Highest Peaks in New England. A Certified Public Accountant and Certified Internal Auditor, Nancy is a graduate of the University of Maine. She is the erstwhile Executive Director of the Maine Brain Injury Foundation and a recently retired bank auditor.

Ron, a graduate of the University of Maine, is retired from the Internal Revenue Service. Formerly a Registered Maine Guide, he was active in the AMC as canoe chair and a trip leader. Currently, he is president of the PPCS and a frequent trip coordinator. In 1997, he was the 38th person certified by the AMC Four Thousand Footer Committee as having climbed the 100 Highest Peaks in New England in the winter. Ron is a freelance writer who has written an outdoor column for a regional newspaper and is currently a regular contributor to several magazines.

preface

For me, the journey that culminated in this book began more than half a century ago on a family trip to Mount Desert Island in eastern Maine. As we drove the scenic roads of Acadia National Park, I was mesmerized by the magnificent barren peaks that surrounded us. Wistfully, I remarked that I'd like to climb them. My dad, who fought his way through the mountains of Europe during World War II, was not impressed. He had done all of the mountain climbing he intended to do in his lifetime. Decades would pass before I realized my aspiration.

In 1976, while working in northern Maine, I glimpsed for the first time the rugged slopes and majestic outline of Mount Katahdin, Maine's highest and most spectacular mountain. I was instantaneously hooked. When I returned home, I announced my intention to climb to the top. Later that summer, a friend and I ascended the Hunt Trail, navigated through thick storm clouds, and reached the summit of Baxter Peak, the high point. Despite poor visibility and cold, windy weather, the experience was thoroughly thrilling. My wife, Nancy, followed a couple of months later. Climbing the mountains of New England has been a significant part of our lives ever since.

The peaks of New England offer great diversity and something for every climbing enthusiast. The Presidentials, Katahdin Range, and Franconia Ridge provide alpine experiences that can challenge the hardiest of mountaineers. The coastal summits of Maine furnish unparalleled panoramic shoreline vistas and outstanding opportunities for bird-watching. Wildlife is abundant in the remote, mountainous regions of western Maine and northern New Hampshire and Vermont, where encounters with deer or moose are not unusual. Quiet hikes through ancient conifer forests supply solace for those seeking solitude and tranquility.

New England enjoys four distinct seasons. Winter brings harsh, cold, snowy weather to the mountains, which can rival arctic conditions at higher elevations. Melting snow, rising streams, and blooming flowers in alpine meadows announce the arrival of spring. Warm, humid weather with extended hours of daylight make spending long days in the cool mountain air particularly appealing during the summer months. Fall ushers in the brilliant colors of autumn and colder temperatures that are ideal for strenuous mountain adventures.

Our book endeavors to provide readers with our version of the finest 30 mountain hikes in New England. Based on our personal experience, we selected the best trails on the most scenic and spectacular mountains. Whenever possible, we chose the easiest routes with the best views.

Writing this book has been a labor of love. Nancy and I revisited peaks and relived decades of memories while enjoying fresh mountain adventures. We developed new skills, even learned to operate a GPS, which we had steadfastly avoided in the past. The process reminded us that we've been blessed with the opportunity to live out our passion for the outdoors in a wonderful mountain playground. We hope this book provides others with a similar experience.

—*Ron Chase*

mountain
recommendations

introduction

This book is intended to provide hikers with a varied selection of the finest mountain hikes in New England. The goal is to supply detailed information on the best scenic trails to the most picturesque and majestic summits. The climbs vary from easy to moderately difficult, but a reasonably fit person who is sufficiently motivated should be able to complete all of the recommended hikes.

There is at least one suggested hike in each New England state. However, since the vast majority of New England's mountains are located in Maine, New Hampshire, and Vermont, those states have a much greater representation in this book. The authors recently completed all of the hikes, and most of the trails are in good shape, obvious, and marked with signs and blazes. That being said, trail conditions change over time, paths are rerouted, signs fall, and blazes fade away. Since all recommended climbs are on relatively popular trails to well-known summits, minor changes or deficiencies should not markedly diminish the quality of the hiking experience.

How to Navigate the Mountains Using This Guidebook

Each climbing profile has a **Key Information** component, which provides specific details regarding the hike, such as length, difficulty, elevation gain, exposure issues, estimated climbing time, and additional data pertinent to that particular trip. The difficulty-rating system separates the climbs into three categories: easy, moderate, and moderately difficult. The two major determinants of the relative difficulty of a hike are length and elevation gain. However, other features, such as particularly steep sections of trail or significant rock, ledge, or boulder scrambling, are also factored into the equation. Estimated climbing times are computed assuming a modest pace with a few short rest stops and a lunch break on longer hikes.

Precise directions to the trailhead from a major intersection in or near the closest significant community are furnished in a separate section called **Directions**. The **In Brief** segment offers an abbreviated synopsis of the major aspects of the trek.

The **Description** provides in-depth analysis of the entire hike, including significant waypoints such as trail junctions, viewpoints, and landmarks. The precise location of the trailhead is furnished, trail conditions described, and the surrounding environment meticulously related. Objective dangers and potential hazards identified by the authors during their hikes are discussed. Out-and-back descriptions detail the climb from the trailhead to the summit, whereas loop hikes and traverses are comprehensively reported from beginning to end. Items of historical note, pertinent weather issues, prime hiking times, and lodging options are discussed in the **History, Weather, and Lodging** portion.

Each hike includes a map with waypoints and an elevation profile. The distances are based on GPS tracking and the use of Delorme software. The authors observed that there is generally some variance between the distances they calculated and those listed on trail signs.

GPS Trailhead Coordinates

To collect accurate map data, each trail was hiked with a handheld GPS unit (Garmin eTrex series). Data collected was then downloaded and plotted onto a digital USGS topo map. In addition to rendering a highly specific trail outline, this book also includes the GPS coordinates for each trailhead in two formats: latitude/longitude and Universal Transverse Mercator (UTM). Latitude/longitude coordinates tell you where you are by locating a point west (latitude) of the 0-degree meridian line that passes through Greenwich, England, and north or south of the 0-degree (longitude) line that belts the earth, aka the equator.

Topographic maps show latitude/longitude as well as UTM grid lines. Known as UTM coordinates, the numbers index a specific point using a grid method. The survey datum used to arrive at the coordinates in this book is WGS84 (versus NAD27 or WGS83). For readers who own a GPS unit, whether handheld or on board a vehicle, the latitude/longitude or UTM coordinates provided on the first page of each climb may be entered into the GPS unit. Just make sure your GPS unit is set to navigate using WGS84 datum. Now you can navigate directly to the trailhead.

Most trailheads, which begin in parking areas, can be reached by car, but some hikes still require a short walk to reach the trailhead from a parking area. In those cases, a handheld unit is necessary to continue the GPS navigation process. That said, however, readers can easily access all trailheads in this book by using the directions given, the overview map, and the trail map, which shows at least one major road leading into the area. But for those who enjoy using the latest GPS technology to navigate, the necessary data has been provided. To learn more about how to enhance your outdoor experiences with GPS technology, refer to *GPS Outdoors: A Practical Guide for Outdoor Enthusiasts* (Menasha Ridge Press).

Safety Issues

Probably the greatest danger encountered on a mountain adventure is the drive to and from the trailhead. However, as with any activity, potential hazards exist. Climbers are encouraged to carry sufficient safety equipment, gear, and supplies to address issues unique to a particular hike and anticipated weather conditions. Mandatory items include a map and compass, plenty of water (Key Information provides recommended amounts per person), food, spare clothing, protective outer gear, headgear, first-aid kit, sunscreen, bug repellent, headlight and batteries, and mittens or gloves. Other items to consider are cell phones and a GPS. Always treat and purify water obtained from streams, rivers, and other outdoor sources.

Before embarking on a climb, inform someone of your destination and anticipated time of return. Be forewarned that climbing alone substantially increases risks. If you become lost and cannot navigate to safety, the general rule of thumb is to remain where you are and wait for help. Hikers should know how to use a map and compass; it is not sufficient to simply carry them. The authors recommend formal orienteering training.

Severe weather is often a possibility in the mountains. Storms or heavy cloud cover can reduce visibility to a few feet and be very disorienting, making good orienteering skills essential. Hypothermia, an abnormally low body temperature, can occur even in the summer months in the mountains. Always take spare warm clothes and obtain a current mountain weather forecast prior to a climb. This is particularly important on hikes with extended above–tree line exposure.

Slips and falls are always a hazard in the mountains. Avoid wet and slippery rocks, ledges, and tree roots. Use particular caution when navigating close to cliffs and precipitous drops. Streams should not be crossed in periods of high water. If there is no clear route across a body of water, turn back.

Ticks have become more common in New England in recent years. Climbers should check their bodies and remove any ticks. If ticks cannot be removed or are believed to have been embedded for extended periods, you should seek professional medical assistance as soon as possible. No wild animals that naturally prey on humans live in New England. However, bears are unpredictable and can be especially dangerous if hikers get between a mother bear and her cub. Hikers should familiarize themselves with techniques for avoiding and dealing with bear encounters.

Enjoying the Outdoors Responsibly

Enjoy wildlife without disturbing it. Always protect the environment. Practice a carry-in and carry-out policy and never leave litter and trash behind. Whenever possible, use trailhead and campsite toilets. If none are available, bury human waste in a six-inch pit well away from sources of water.

Respect the rights of private landowners. All recommended hikes in this book are on trails open to the public. However, some cross private lands, and many are adjacent to private property.

1. BEAR MOUNTAIN

CONNECTICUT

01 *Bear Mountain*

UNDERMOUNTAIN AND APPALACHIAN TRAILS

GPS Trailhead Coordinates

UTM Zone (WGS 84)	18T
Easting	0630023.4
Northing	4653945.3
Latitude	N 42° 01'43.71"
Longitude	W 73° 25'44.14"

🥾 Key Information

LENGTH 5.16 miles

ROUTE CONFIGURATION Out-and-back

DIFFICULTY Easy to moderate

ELEVATION GAIN 1,547 feet

SCENERY Outstanding views of the mountains of northwestern Connecticut and beyond

EXPOSURE Some exposure to the elements

TRAIL TRAFFIC Heavy

TRAIL SURFACE Hard-packed dirt and rock with some ledge scrambling

CLIMBING TIME 4 hours

DRIVING DISTANCE Approximately 60 miles from the junction of Interstate 84 and CT 8 in Waterbury, CT

ACCESS No fees or permits required

MAPS USGS Quadrangle for Ashley Falls

FACILITIES Primitive toilet at the trailhead

WATER REQUIREMENT 1.5 quarts per person recommended

DOGS ALLOWED Yes

ELEVATION PROFILE

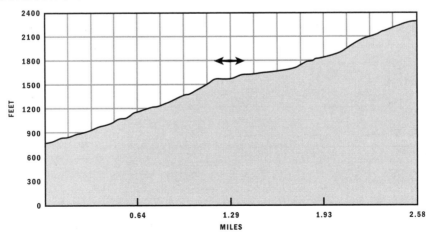

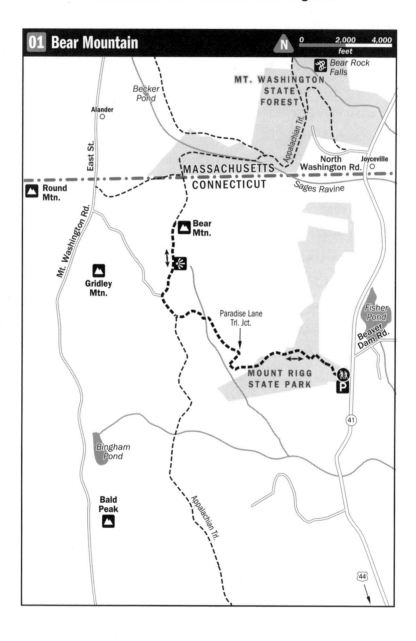

Stone pyramid at the summit of Bear Mountain

Directions

From the intersection of I-84 and CT 8 in Waterbury, CT, drive north on CT 8 19.5 miles to CT 4 in Torrington. Go west on CT 4 15 miles to CT 7 in Cornwall Bridge. Turn right and drive 14.5 miles north to US 44 on the left in Canaan. Go left and continue 6.6 miles to CT 41 in Salisbury. Drive north on CT 41 3.3 miles to a parking area on the left. The trailhead is in the right rear corner of the parking area, next to a large rock.

In Brief

Bear Mountain, elevation 2,316 feet, is the highest peak in Connecticut. The summit and partially exposed south ridge provide exceptional views of the Berkshire Mountains of Connecticut and Massachusetts and the Catskills of New York. The Undermountain and Appalachian trails to the summit are easy-to-moderate in difficulty, with some ledge scrambling at higher elevations.

Trail sign at Riga Junction on the Appalachian Trail near Bear Mountain

Description

From the right rear corner of the parking area, walk past a large rock with a blue blaze painted on the front, under a wooden "trail" sign posted on a tree. Go 30 yards beneath tall hardwood trees to the trailhead for the Undermountain Trail next to an information kiosk. A spur trail to the left leads 50 yards through a wooded area to a primitive toilet.

Ascend gradually in a westerly direction on a good hard-packed dirt path with some tree-root exposure in a predominantly hardwood forest. Angle sharply right at 1 mile and persist steadily upward under lofty, overhanging elm and maple trees until you reach the junction with Paradise Lane Trail on the right at 1.2 miles.

Turn left, drop down, and hike easily on an obvious footpath. At 1.5 miles, enter a low wet and muddy area and negotiate a series of narrow boardwalks. Begin climbing more steadily at 1.8 miles and reach Riga Junction on the Appalachian Trail at 1.9 miles. The junction is marked with a significant trail sign that provides mileage information for various destinations north and south.

Turn right on the Appalachian Trail and follow white blazes on a well-defined route to a "trail" sign posted on a tree at 2 miles. Avoid an unmarked path to the left and bear right at the sign. Climb steeply on a boulder and rock–strewn surface to a rock lookout on the left at 2.2 miles. Scale the huge boulder and savor the excellent panoramic vistas of the Catskills of New York in the west.

Recommence ascending steadily on a rocky surface in stunted mountain vegetation with sporadic views south and west. At 2.4 miles, reach an extended, sloping ledge facing southwest, which provides phenomenal views of mountainous northwestern Connecticut. Persist on a partially exposed ridge in a patchy scrub for 0.2 miles to the summit, marked with a large stone pyramid.

Climb the slanted, rectangular-shaped pyramid for spectacular views in all directions. The Berkshires of northern Connecticut and western Massachusetts dominate the northern landscape, and the Catskills of New York command the western horizon. The lakes and hills of the Connecticut countryside are visible to the south and east. The roof of the pyramid is the perfect spot for a prolonged, leisurely lunch break. Descend the ridge while enjoying continuous views south, then resume downward on the Appalachian Trail to Riga Junction and return to the Undermountain trailhead.

The Appalachian Trail is the primary mountaineering objective in the Bear Mountain area. Access points are located in Salisbury, Falls Village, West Cornwall, and Cornwall Bridge. Side trails also connect with the Appalachian Trail, including Paradise Lane Trail north of Bear Mountain and Pine Knob Loop Trail near Cornwall Bridge.

History, Weather, and Lodging

Bear Mountain is the highest peak located in Connecticut and reputed to be its most popular hike. A plaque embedded in the stone-pyramid summit marker states, "This monument marks the highest ground in Connecticut 2,334 feet above sea, built AD 1885 Owen Travis Mason." However, the true summit elevation is now believed to be 2,316 feet, and the highest ground in Connecticut is 2,380 feet, located on the south slope of Mount Frissell, a few miles away. The summit of Mount Frissell, at 2,453 feet, lies in Massachusetts.

The ascent on the Undermountain Trail to Riga Junction is below tree line. However, much of the remaining climb on the Appalachian Trail to the summit of Bear Mountain is exposed to the elements. Be prepared for wind, rain, sun, and cold in this area. Spring, summer, and fall are good seasons for a hike on Bear Mountain.

Several hotels, motels, and bed-and-breakfasts are located in nearby Salisbury, Lakeville, and Canaan. The Housatonic Meadows State Park in Cornwall, about 20 miles south on CT 7, is an excellent camping choice. Some hiking gear and supplies can be purchased in Salisbury.

MAINE

02   *Pleasant Mountain*
SOUTHWEST RIDGE TRAIL

GPS Trailhead Coordinates

UTM Zone (WGS 84)	19T
Easting	0351357.6
Northing	4874110.4
Latitude	N 44° 00'25.60"
Longitude	W 70° 51'13.15"

𝑨𝑨 Key Information

LENGTH 4.86 miles

ROUTE CONFIGURATION Out-and-back

DIFFICULTY Easy

ELEVATION GAIN 1,169 feet

SCENERY Excellent views of western Maine's mountains and lakes and New Hampshire's White Mountains

EXPOSURE Some exposure to the elements on an open ridge and the summit area

TRAIL TRAFFIC Moderate

TRAIL SURFACE Rock and dirt

CLIMBING TIME 4 hours

DRIVING DISTANCE 45.7 miles from Interstate 95 and US 302 in Portland, ME

ACCESS No fees or permits required

MAPS USGS Quadrangle for Pleasant Mountain

FACILITIES None

WATER REQUIREMENT 1.5 quarts per person recommended

DOGS ALLOWED Yes

ELEVATION PROFILE

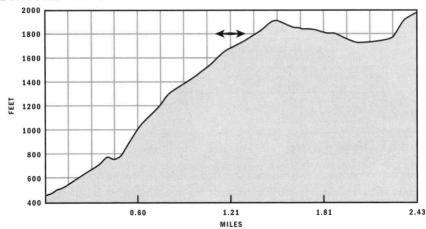

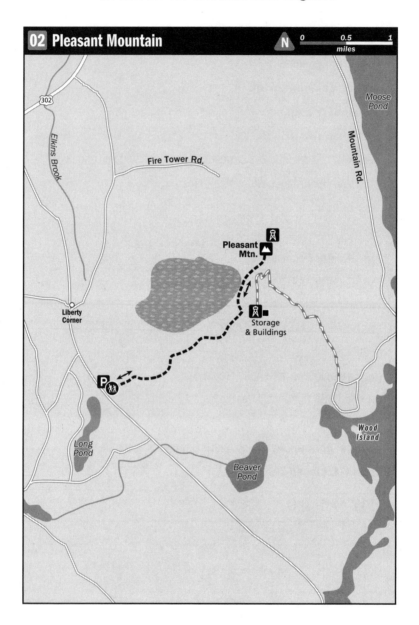

Directions

From the intersection of I-95 and US 302 in Portland, ME, follow US 302 8.6 miles to an intersection with US 202 in Windham Center. Continue on US 302 34.3 miles through North

Hikers descend the Southwest Ridge Trail with Pleasant Pond below.

Windham, Naples, and Bridgton to Denmark Road in East Fryeburg. Turn left on Denmark Road, a dirt road in good condition, and drive 1.9 miles to an intersection where Harnden Road exits right and Wilton Warren Road exits left. Continue straight onto Lake Road and drive 0.9 miles to an unmarked parking area on the left. The trailhead is located in the far left rear corner of the parking area.

In Brief

Pleasant Mountain, located in the Lakes Region of southwestern Maine, is home to Shawnee Peak Ski Resort, which dominates the north side of the mountain and overlooks US 302 and the surrounding area. It is the highest mountain in southern Maine and a prominent landmark. Most of the hike lies inside Pleasant Mountain Preserve, and the Southwest Ridge Trail and summit area provide excellent views of the area's mountains and lakes and New Hampshire's White Mountains. It is an easy hike to the summit at an elevation of 2,006 feet.

A hiker enjoys a view of Moose Pond from the Southwest Ridge Trail.

Description

From the trailhead for Southwest Ridge Trail (also known as MacKay Pasture Trail), hike northeast on a gentle grade through a hardwood forest for 0.5 miles to a small cairn. Turn sharply to the right and hike southeasterly for 100 yards to an open ledge overlooking Beaver and Moose ponds.

The trail parallels Moose Pond for the remainder of the hike to south peak. Edge along the precipitous cliffs of the mountain's south face and follow the cairns, climbing steadily up exposed ledges for 1 mile to a high point on the ridge. Drop slightly in elevation and walk along a nearly flat crest in a canopy of hardwoods to an obvious, but unmarked, trail junction on the right at 1.9 miles. Here, the trail has been recently rerouted to the left.

The former trail is now a 0.2-mile spur path leading to the summit of the southernmost peak on the mountain. A communications tower is located on top, and a cliff nearby points south and affords an extensive view of Moose Pond. Beyond the tower is a messy, muddy road leading north and then east to the village of Denmark; avoid this road.

From the spur trail junction, descend gradually through a wooded area to the saddle between South Peak and the summit. At 2.2 miles, the trail switchbacks to the left and climbs steeply for 0.1 mile and then more gradually for another 0.1 mile to the summit. A closed fire tower and a couple of small storage buildings sit at the summit. Turn west and walk about 100 feet to cliffs that provide panoramic vistas of the Mahoosuc Mountains of western Maine and the White Mountains of New Hampshire. On a clear day, this location provides spectacular views of majestic Mount Washington and the alpine peaks of the Presidential Range, often snow-covered into late spring and again beginning in the fall.

Three additional trails converge near the summit. Fire Warden's Trail arrives from the northwest; it's a wet, dank path with muddy roads intersecting it, and I do not recommend it. Bald Peak and Ledges trails both start on the east side of the mountain. A traverse of either in conjunction with the Southwest Ridge Trail would necessitate a long shuttle on dirt and secondary roads. Trailheads for both are located on Mountain Road, a left turn 0.4 miles west of the causeway over Moose Pond on US 302. Neither trail offers the extensive views provided by Southwest Ridge Trail, and both tend to be wet as they parallel streams. Bald Peak Trail is poorly marked and difficult to follow, particularly at lower elevations where the trail is badly eroded. An out-and-back hike on Southwest Ridge Trail is the best option.

Drop to the saddle and hike around South Peak to the ledges of the Southwest Ridge. Descend the steep path, exercising caution on the rocky granite boulders, which can be slippery when wet. Enjoy the almost continuous views to the west on the return trip to the parking area. A late-afternoon hike can often culminate with a breathtaking sunset.

History, Weather, and Lodging

Pleasant Mountain has been a popular hiking destination for decades. In recent years, concerns about potential development of the mountain prompted efforts to protect this recreational and ecological treasure. The Loon Echo Land Trust recently organized a fundraising campaign that resulted in the creation of the Pleasant Mountain Preserve. The preserve currently consists of about 1,500 acres of land purchases and easements that include most of the mountain's east side and much of Southwest Ridge Trail. Efforts are under way to expand the size of the preserve.

Loon Echo volunteers currently maintain the trails in the preserve. There are additional plans to build kiosks, erect trail signs, and post trail maps. Trail crews will attempt to reverse the effects of years of trail erosion.

Free of brooks and streams, Southwest Ridge Trail is normally a good hike during spring, summer, or fall. You may experience modest exposure to sun, wind, rain, and cold while ascending the ridge; however, you can quickly minimize those conditions by seeking shelter in wooded areas nearby. Pleasant Mountain is a popular destination for leaf peepers in late September. Bird-watchers also frequent its trails.

Scores of motels, hotels, and bed-and-breakfasts are located along US 302 between Portland and Pleasant Mountain. Nearby towns of Fryeburg and Bridgton provide several lodging establishments, and numerous campgrounds are available in this popular vacation destination area.

03 *Tumbledown Mountain*
PARKER RIDGE AND TUMBLEDOWN RIDGE TRAILS TO EAST PEAK

GPS Trailhead Coordinates

UTM Zone (WGS 84)	19T
Easting	0379989.9
Northing	4954337.2
Latitude	N 44° 44'3.76"
Longitude	W 70° 30'54.50"

🥾 Key Information

LENGTH 4.34 miles

ROUTE CONFIGURATION Out-and-back

DIFFICULTY Moderate

ELEVATION GAIN Excess of 1,850 feet

SCENERY Extended above–tree line views of Webb Lake and surrounding mountains

EXPOSURE Above–tree line exposure to the elements

TRAIL TRAFFIC Moderate

TRAIL SURFACE Dirt and ledge below tree line and rock and granite ledges above

CLIMBING TIME 5 hours

DRIVING DISTANCE 60 miles from the junction of Interstate 95 and ME 27 in Augusta

ACCESS No fees or permits required

MAPS USGS Quadrangles for Roxbury and Jackson Mountain

FACILITIES None

WATER REQUIREMENT 1.5 quarts per person

DOGS ALLOWED Yes

ELEVATION PROFILE

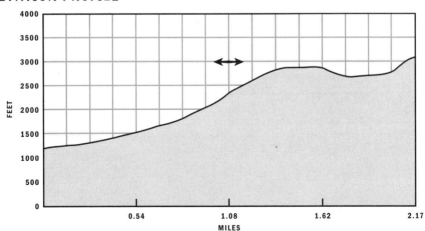

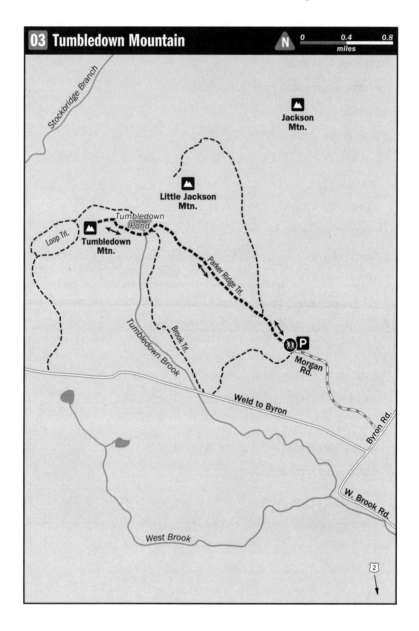

03 **Tumbledown Mountain**

N   0   0.4   0.8
                miles

Jackson
Mtn.

Stockbridge Branch

Little Jackson
Mtn.

Tumbledown
Pond

Loop Trl.

Tumbledown
Mtn.

Parker Ridge Trl.

P

Morgan
Rd.

Tumbledown Brook

Brook Trl.

Weld to Byron

Byron Rd.

W. Brook Rd.

West Brook

2

Hikers ascend Parker Ridge Trail.

Directions

From the intersection of I-95 and ME 27 in Augusta, follow ME 27 24.2 miles to the junction with US 2 in New Sharon. Turn left on US 2 and drive 9.7 miles to Farmington. Turn left on US 2 and ME 4 and drive 8 miles to ME 156 in Wilton. Turn right and continue north on ME 156 11.8 miles to ME 142 in Weld. Go straight on ME 142 for 2.4 miles and turn left on the Byron Road. Take an immediate right turn on a dirt road that is in good condition, and drive 2.5 miles to a narrow dirt road on the right just after an old cemetery. Follow this rough-but-passable road, which may require a four-wheel or all-wheel-drive vehicle, 1.2 miles to where it dead-ends in a parking area. The trailhead is on the north side of the parking area.

In Brief

Located in western Maine, Tumbledown Mountain is one of Maine's most popular hikes. With its three craggy, barren alpine peaks dominating the landscape, it is also one of the most distinctive mountains in Maine. At an elevation of 3,088 feet, it is not a particularly tall mountain, but a hike to the summit of East Peak is moderate in difficulty. There is some hand-over-hand rock scrambling just before emerging above tree line, and you should expect significant exposure to cold, wind, sun, and rain in the extensive alpine zone. The higher elevations offer outstanding views of the mountains and lakes of the region.

Hikers skirt cliffs on Tumbledown Ridge Trail on a cold fall day.

Description

From the trailhead, hike the Parker Ridge Trail on a gentle grade along the remains of an old logging road for 0.3 miles to the Little Jackson Mountain Trail junction on the right. Pay particular attention to trail signs, cairns, and trail blazes early on, as there are several old roads in this area that appear to be hiking trails. Adding to the confusion, mountain torrents have badly eroded this section of path and there has been some rerouting of trails in recent years. The trail system on Tumbledown Mountain has a reputation for being perplexing; use of a map, compass, and GPS is advisable.

Continue 0.7 miles through a sparse forest of conifers and mixed hardwoods to a series of ledges that rise precipitously. Ascend steeply to the tree line in an area where some hand-over-hand rock scrambling is required. Emerge above tree line and traverse the huge granite boulders of Parker Ridge. At 1.6 miles drop abruptly to an alpine tarn called Tumbledown Pond. Brook Trail departs to the south just a few yards before reaching the pond.

Tumbledown Pond is immersed in alpine beauty, as Little Jackson Mountain and the peaks of Tumbledown surround it. Backpackers often camp along the shore, and the State of Maine Inland Fisheries and Game Department stocks the pond with trout. Fishing is permitted, but a Maine fishing license is required.

Follow the Tumbledown Ridge Trail westerly along the shore of the pond and then climb arduously on the exposed-rock face of East Peak. Scramble over the boulders 0.6 miles to the summit. Exercise caution on the ridge, particularly when it is wet, as some sections are perilously close to the sheer cliffs of the south face. Along the ridge there are panoramic views of nearby Webb Lake, Mount Blue, and the peaks of the Tumbledown Range. Be prepared for cool, brisk winds that blow from the north and chill the air on the barren ridge and summit. Be alert for opportunities to view the endangered peregrine falcons that nest in the nearby cliffs.

On the return, use care descending the steep ledges of East Peak and Parker Ridge, as a misstep could result in an unpleasant fall. The Loop and Brook trails also descend from near the summit of Tumbledown to the Byron Road. Neither is recommended as they are poorly marked, steep, and wet.

History, Weather, and Lodging

There is a history of land-ownership changes on Tumbledown Mountain. In recent years, there have been growing concerns that continued private ownership could lead to restricted access, development, or heavy logging. A campaign was launched in 1999 to preserve the mountain. Spearheaded by the Tumbledown Conservation Alliance, a coalition of organizations, local groups, and individuals, the campaign has made substantial progress. The State of Maine and its partners have been successful in securing the summit area and northern slopes of Tumbledown and close-by Little Jackson and Blueberry Mountains. Efforts persist to protect the southern slopes, where most of the hiking trails are located.

There are several additional hiking opportunities in the Tumbledown Mountain region. Little Jackson Mountain can be ascended by climbing north after hiking 0.3 miles on the Parker Ridge Trail. Nearby Mount Blue is an easy-to-moderate hike, and there are several short, easy hikes in Mount Blue State Park.

The weather on Tumbledown can be cold and windy, particularly in the fall, when snow, sleet, and freezing rain storms are also a threat. Prior to climbing, obtain a reliable mountain weather forecast. The best times to hike on Tumbledown are during the summer and early fall. The varied brilliant colors of autumn are generally at their peak in late September or the beginning of October.

Tumbledown Mountain is located in a remote location, and lodging options are negligible in the proximate area. There are a few motels in Farmington, about 25 miles away. Mount Blue State Park offers an excellent camping option on beautiful Webb Lake in the shadows of Tumbledown.

04   *Ragged Mountain*
          GEORGES HIGHLAND PATH

GPS Trailhead Coordinates

UTM Zone (WGS 84)	19T
Easting	0487322.8
Northing	4994080.5
Latitude	N 44° 12'6.62"
Longitude	W 69° 09'29.31"

🚶 Key Information

LENGTH 5.4 miles

ROUTE CONFIGURATION Out-and-back

DIFFICULTY Easy

ELEVATION GAIN 870 feet

SCENERY Exceptional views of Penobscot Bay and surrounding Camden Hills

EXPOSURE Some exposure to the elements

TRAIL TRAFFIC Moderate to heavy

TRAIL SURFACE Dirt and granite ledge

CLIMBING TIME 4 hours

DRIVING DISTANCE 54.3 miles from the intersection of Interstate 295 and ME 196 in Topsham, ME

ACCESS No fees or permits required

MAPS USGS Quadrangle for West Rockport

FACILITIES None

WATER REQUIREMENT 1 quart per person recommended

DOGS ALLOWED Yes

ELEVATION PROFILE

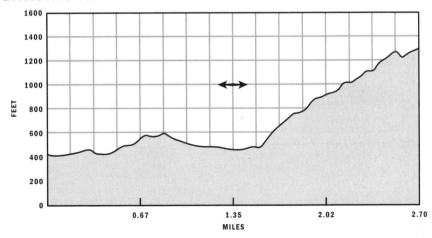

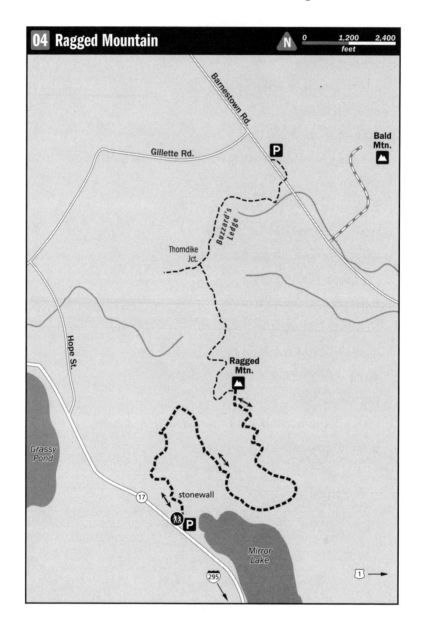

04 Ragged Mountain

N   0   1,200   2,400
feet

Barnestown Rd.

Gillette Rd.

Bald Mtn.

Buzzard's Ledge

Thorndike Jct.

Hope St.

Ragged Mtn.

Grassy Pond

17

stonewall

Mirror Lake

295

1 →

Directions

From the intersection of I-295 and ME 196 in Topsham, ME, follow ME 196 east 2 miles to US 1 in Brunswick. Drive north on US 1 through Bath and Wiscasset 42 miles to ME 90 in Warren. Travel east on ME 90 8.4 miles to ME 17 in West Rockport. Turn left and drive 1.9 miles west on ME 17 (past Mirror Lake on the right) to a parking area on the right in a stand of pines. The trailhead for Georges Highland Path to Ragged Mountain is at the left end of the parking area.

In Brief

Located just 4 miles from beautiful Penobscot Bay in midcoast Maine, Ragged Mountain (elevation 1,288 feet) provides spectacular panoramic views of Rockland and Rockport harbors and dozens of offshore islands. Cliffs along its rugged south face overlook scenic Mirror Lake and Pleasant and Spruce mountains beyond. It sits near the southern terminus of a range of small coastal mountains called Camden Hills. The recently developed trail system is well marked and in good condition.

Description

From the trailhead, traverse a low, wet area and then hike easily on the Georges Highland Path in a northerly direction through a new growth of conifers and hardwoods. At 0.1 mile, cross the remnants of a stone wall built by early European settlers to corral livestock and define boundaries. This stone wall once extended for more than 30 miles through the midcoast Maine region.

At 0.8 miles reach the base of the cliffs on the south face of Ragged Mountain. Turn southeast and hike along the foot of the cliffs on a rocky, uneven trail until the northern tip of Mirror Lake becomes visible at 1.4 miles. After another 0.1 mile, veer sharply to the northeast and begin a steady ascent on a hard-packed dirt path. At 1.8 miles swing to the northwest past a large rock formation partially concealed by low-growth vegetation and edge along the cliffs on the south face, continuing steadily upward. Here, enjoy sporadic glimpses of aptly named Mirror Lake reflecting up from below. Reach a granite overlook at 2.2 miles with unobstructed views of Spruce and Pleasant mountains to the south and Grassy Pond to the west.

Leave the overlook, turn right, and enter a stand of predominantly white birch trees. At 2.5 miles emerge from the forested area onto a wide, exposed ledge that faces east and provides expansive views of island-speckled Penobscot Bay. Though the large islands of North Haven, Vinalhaven, Islesboro, and Isle au Haut are more than 20 miles away, you can easily observe them from this vantage point on most days. Frequently, you may also see ferries motoring to and from the mainland.

Scramble northwesterly along steep ledges on the south face for 0.1 mile. Take an unmarked but obvious path that leaves the main trail on the right and climb over large boulders to the summit. From the top, you'll enjoy glorious views to the south and west, and much of the upper south face is visible immediately below. Walk around to the right of a small

Hikers nearing the summit of Ragged Mountain

communications complex and find ledges that overlook Penobscot Bay in the east. The summit is an excellent location to stop, rest, and enjoy a picnic lunch. Descend carefully on the steep ledges to the main trail and return to the parking area on ME 17.

A traverse of Ragged Mountain is also possible by continuing on the Georges Highland Path, but a shuttle is required. To set up a shuttle, drive west from the ME 17 parking lot for 0.7 miles to Hope Street on the right. Follow Hope Street for 1 mile to the intersection with Gillette Road. Turn right and continue 1.4 miles to Barnstown Road. Turn right and go 100 yards to a small parking area on the left.

To complete the traverse, hike west from the junction with the summit spur trail along the south face cliffs following cairns for 0.2 miles, and drop into a narrow ravine. Climb out of the cleft and cross an exposed ledge. Enter mountain scrub and scramble over some boulders for 0.1 mile. At 0.4 miles, drop into a thinly wooded area and hike easily for 0.6 miles to the Thorndike Junction, identified by a large wooden sign.

At the junction, a trail to the left leads to the Thorndike Brook Access. Avoid what appears to be a trail leading straight ahead, as it dead-ends on private property. Instead, turn right and go 0.1 mile and ascend slightly to Buzzard's Ledge at 1.2 miles. The open ledge faces northeast and affords an excellent view of nearby Bald Mountain.

Descend the steep ledge and then hike down a hard-packed dirt trail through a mostly conifer forest for 0.6 miles to Barnstown Road at 1.8 miles. Cross the road and hike steadily up a damp, rocky path that parallels the road for 0.2 miles to the parking area.

Several additional hikes on Georges Highland Path are options in the western sector of the Camden Hills. On the opposite side of the road from the ME 17 trailhead parking area, the path travels west along the northern slopes of Spruce and Pleasant mountains for 4.5 miles. A 2.2-mile summit loop hike over Bald Mountain begins at the Barnstown Road Access parking area and travels northeast. Finally, the Thorndike Brook Access on Hope Street provides an alternative approach to Ragged Mountain.

History, Weather, and Lodging

Georges Highland Path is a relatively new trail system developed by the Georges River Land Trust. Consisting of more than 35 miles of trails, the path meanders through the Camden Hills of midcoast Maine. The trust protects more than 1,000 acres in the region and advocates a "conservation trails" concept. A nonprofit organization founded by local citizens in 1987, the trust encourages preservation of the Georges River watershed region. For more information on the organization, access their Web site at www.grlt.org.

You'll experience some exposure to sun, rain, wind, and cold on the cliffs of the south face and summit area of Ragged Mountain. Given their proximity to the ocean, the Camden Hills experience a maritime weather pattern, which often includes damp, foggy, and windy conditions. Hikers should be prepared for those circumstances during any season. Normally, spring, summer, and fall are all good seasons to climb Ragged Mountain. The colorful autumn foliage usually peaks near the end of September.

Numerous resorts, hotels, motels, and bed-and-breakfasts are available in nearby Rockland and Rockport. In addition, several private campgrounds operate in the area, and Camden Hills State Park in Camden has a large selection of campsites. A number of businesses in the area sell hiking and climbing supplies and gear.

05   *Mount Megunticook*
MEGUNTICOOK AND NATURE TRAILS LOOP

GPS Trailhead Coordinates

UTM Zone (WGS 84)	19T
Easting	0496011
Northing	4897234.6
Latitude	N 44° 13'49.21"
Longitude	W 69° 02'57.95"

🥾 Key Information

LENGTH 3.48 miles

ROUTE CONFIGURATION Loop with an out-and-back summit hike

DIFFICULTY Easy

ELEVATION GAIN 1,169 feet

SCENERY Phenomenal views of Camden Harbor and Penobscot Bay

EXPOSURE Modest exposure to the elements

TRAIL TRAFFIC Heavy

TRAIL SURFACE Dirt and rock ledges

CLIMBING TIME 3 hours

DRIVING DISTANCE 58.5 miles from the junction of I-295 and ME 196 in Topsham, ME

ACCESS Nominal day-use fee

MAPS USGS Quadrangle for Camden

FACILITIES Primitive toilets at parking areas

WATER REQUIREMENT 1 quart per person recommended

DOGS ALLOWED Yes

ELEVATION PROFILE

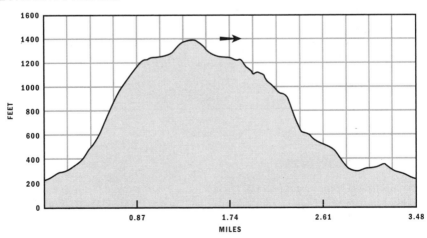

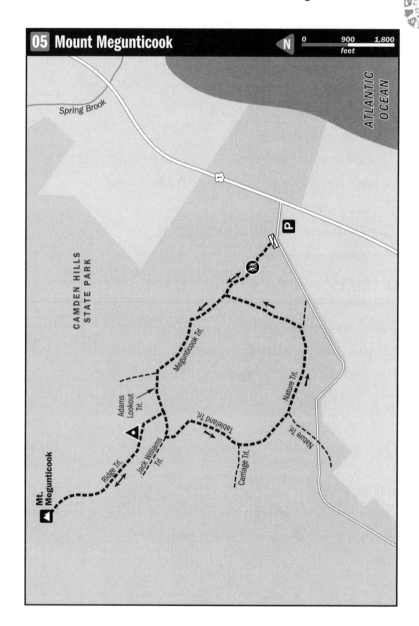

Directions

From the intersection of I-295 and ME 196 in Topsham, ME, follow ME 196 east 2 miles to US 1 in Brunswick. Drive north on US 1 through Bath and Wiscasset 42 miles to ME 90 in Warren.

Hikers arrive at Ocean Overlook with busy Camden Harbor in the background.

Travel east on ME 90 10.8 miles to US 1 in Rockport. Drive north on US 1 through Camden 3.7 miles to Camden Hills State Park on the left. Immediately after entering the park, bear left to a large parking area across the road from the park gate and tollhouse. The trailhead is 0.2 miles straight up the park road beyond the tollhouse.

In Brief

"Where the mountains meet the sea" is an oft-quoted phrase attributed to poet Edna St. Vincent Millay to describe the Camden Hills. Located in Camden Hills State Park in midcoast Maine, Mount Megunticook is the tallest of the Camden Hills, at an elevation of 1,385 feet. According to park literature, it is also the "highest mainland mountain on the Atlantic coast." Ocean Overlook on Ridge Trail provides some of the most phenomenal ocean vistas found anywhere in Maine.

A hiker studies beautiful Megunticook Lake from the cliffs of Mount Megunticook—leaves are beginning to turn colors.

Description

From the tollhouse gate, walk straight up the park road for 0.2 miles to the trailhead for Megunticook Trail. Cross a shallow brook and hike gently for 0.1 mile on an often wet but well-marked path to the Nature Trail junction on the left. Continue gradually on Megunticook Trail via long switchbacks through a sparse hardwood forest that provides continuous, slightly obstructed views of Penobscot Bay. Turn abruptly to the left onto Adam's Lookout Trail at 0.7 miles and hike southwest for 100 yards to open ledges where expansive views of the bay await. Follow the cairns and climb steadily up the ledges and through a thinly forested area to a junction with Tablelands and Ridge trails at 0.8 miles. Turn right on Ridge Trail and scramble steeply up boulders and ledges for 0.2 miles to Ocean Overlook.

Don't forget a camera, as Ocean Overlook has an almost fabled reputation for the views it provides of Camden Harbor and Penobscot Bay. Situated at the top of sheer cliffs facing southwest, hikers can look directly down into picturesque Camden Harbor with tiny Curtis Island Lighthouse guarding the entrance. Beyond, dozens of islands dot spectacular Penobscot Bay.

Often, you can see ferries commuting between the mainland and the large islands of Vinal-haven and North Haven. Imagine a youthful Edna St. Vincent Millay sitting at the edge of the cliffs and contemplating the visual delights, as she most assuredly visited this spot. Megunti-cook cliffs are a popular destination for technical rock climbers; frequently, hikers are surprised by unexpected visitors while standing at the edge of the precipice.

From the overlook, skirt northwest along the cliffs on Ridge Trail while stealing glimpses of beautiful Megunticook Lake. Follow white blazes and turn sharply to the right to enter a dense conifer forest. Hike gradually for 0.4 miles on a wet trail to the high point. Climb over two steep ledges just before reaching the true summit (marked with a large cairn).

Return on Ridge Trail to the overlook and then descend a steep path to the Adam's Look-out Trail junction. Turn right on Tablelands Trail and drop dramatically on a boulder-strewn path for 0.2 miles to the Jack Williams Trail junction at 2.1 miles. Be particularly careful in this area, as the rocks are slippery when wet. At this junction, take time to enjoy a view of the sweeping cliffs of Megunticook to the north. Hike gradually down Tablelands Trail past Car-riage Trail on the right at 2.4 miles and arrive at Nature Trail at 2.6 miles.

Descend easily on the Nature Trail, which shadows the Mount Battie Auto Road for 0.3 miles to a footpath on the right. The footpath leads to an alternate parking area with a primi-tive toilet. Continue on the Nature Trail for an additional 0.3 miles to Megunticook Trail at 3.2 miles. Return to the beginning trailhead and walk down the park road to the parking area.

Hiking opportunities abound in the Camden Hills. More than 30 miles of trails exist in the state park, with trailheads on US 1, ME 52, and Youngstown Road. Using shuttle vehicles, sev-eral traverse options are possible. The Georges Highland Path trail system offers an additional 35 miles of trails outside the park in the western portion of the Camden Hills.

History, Weather, and Lodging

Poet and playwright Edna St. Vincent Millay spent much of her youth living in Camden within sight of the majestic Mount Megunticook cliffs. She is reputed to have enjoyed hiking its trails and those of nearby Mount Battie. In 1912, she catapulted to fame with her poem "Renascence," which captures the essence of the charm and beauty of those mountains and Penobscot Bay. She went on to become the first woman to receive the Pulitzer Prize for Poetry and one of the most famous literary figures of the 20th century.

The Camden Hills experience a maritime atmospheric pattern that frequently includes onshore winds, rain, and foggy weather. Even on warm summer days, hikers should be pre-pared for damp, cool, and breezy circumstances. Hiking conditions are generally favorable from mid-spring through late fall. The Camden Hills attract many seeking the beauty of fall foliage each September.

The midcoast is a destination for vacationers, tourists, and outdoor enthusiasts. An abun-dance of resorts, hotels, motels, and bed-and-breakfasts are in the nearby towns of Camden, Rockport, Rockland, and Lincolnville. Several private campgrounds are available in the area, and Camden Hills State Park has a camping area with 107 sites. Various retailers operate busi-nesses that cater to hikers and climbers in Camden and Rockport.

06

Champlain Mountain
BEACHCROFT TRAIL

GPS Trailhead Coordinates

UTM Zone (WGS 84)	19T	
Easting	0563317.6	
Northing	4911690.2	
Latitude	N 44° 21'27.80"	
Longitude	W 68° 12'17.89"	

🏃 Key Information

LENGTH 1.9 miles

ROUTE CONFIGURATION Out-and-back

DIFFICULTY Easy

ELEVATION GAIN Exceeds 950 feet

SCENERY Spectacular views of Mount Desert Island and Frenchman and Penobscot bays

EXPOSURE Continuous exposure to the elements

TRAIL TRAFFIC Moderate to heavy

TRAIL SURFACE Primarily rock slab and ledge

CLIMBING TIME 2.5 hours

DRIVING DISTANCE 51.8 miles from Interstate 95 and Interstate 395 in Bangor, ME

ACCESS No fees or permits required for an out-and-back hike

MAPS USGS Quadrangle for Seal Harbor

FACILITIES None

WATER REQUIREMENT One quart per person recommended

DOGS ALLOWED Yes

ELEVATION PROFILE

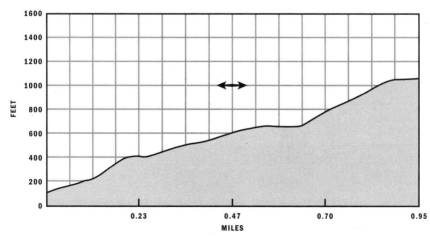

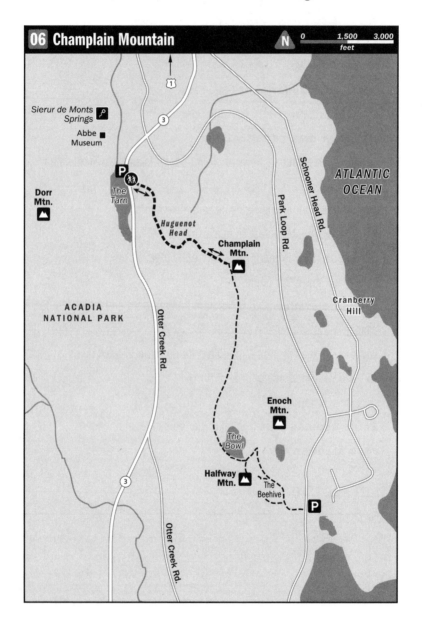

06 **Champlain Mountain**

N

0   1,500   3,000
feet

Sierur de Monts Springs

Abbe Museum

Dorr Mtn.

The Tarn

Huguenot Head

Champlain Mtn.

ATLANTIC OCEAN

Schooner Head Rd.

Park Loop Rd.

ACADIA NATIONAL PARK

Otter Creek Rd.

Cranberry Hill

Enoch Mtn.

The Bowl

Halfway Mtn.

The Beehive

3

3

1

Otter Creek Rd.

Directions

From the intersection of I-95 and I-395 in Bangor, ME, follow I-395 east 5.2 miles to US 1A in Brewer. Continue east on US 1A 23 miles to the junction with US 1 in Ellsworth. Follow US 1 north 1 mile through the Ellsworth business district to the junction with ME 3. Drive straight on ME 3 for 8.4 miles to ME 102 on Mount Desert Island. Turn right on ME 102 and drive 4.3 miles. Turn left on ME 198 and go 1.4 miles. Turn left on ME 233 and travel 5.8 miles to ME 3 in Bar Harbor. Go straight on ME 3 for 2.7 miles to a parking area on the right just before a mountain pond called The Tarn. The trailhead is directly across ME 3 from the parking area and is marked with a sign.

In Brief

Champlain Mountain in Acadia National Park is the easternmost peak on Mount Desert Island. At the summit, unparalleled views of Frenchman Bay, the Porcupine Islands, and Schoodic Peninsula await. Imposing ocean-facing cliffs make it one of the most distinctive and popular hiking mountains on the Maine coast.

Description

From the parking area, watch for traffic and carefully cross ME 3. The trailhead, directly across the road from the south end of the parking area, is marked by a wooden sign. Hike easily on a gentle grade through a stand of white birch trees for 0.1 mile. You'll parallel ME 3 before climbing more steeply on a well-defined rock-strewn trail that quickly gains elevation. Ascend the west side of a granite crag called Huguenot Head via switchbacks. At the same time, look directly down into The Tarn and appreciate the stark views of barren Dorr and Cadillac mountains to the west.

Turn left near the top of Huguenot Head at 0.6 miles and hike east. There is no actual trail here, but it is possible to scramble up a well-worn path to the true high point on the Head. Descend gradually through a dense spruce growth for 0.1 mile to a narrow col before beginning a steady ascent on the exposed west face of Champlain Mountain. Follow cairns and blue blazes southeasterly while traversing huge granite slabs to the summit at 0.95 miles.

The views from the summit of Champlain Mountain are simply unparalleled on a clear day. To the north are Frenchman Bay and the rugged Porcupine Islands. Across the bay in the east is the irregular coastline of Schoodic Peninsula, home to the eastern arm of Acadia National Park. Magnificent Penobscot Bay is visible beyond the south end of the Champlain Mountain summit ridge, and you can observe most of the 16 peaks of Mount Desert Island to the west.

Find shelter in the rocks from any coastal breezes and enjoy a picnic lunch while feasting on the views. Large boulders on the cliffs facing east provide exceptional vantage points. The Precipice Trail, reputed to be the most technically difficult trail in Acadia National Park, climbs the east face and arrives at the summit nearby. However, this trail is often closed during summer to protect the endangered peregrine falcons nesting in the cliffs. Carry binoculars and look for them soaring above Frenchman Bay. On a clear, sunny day, you'll see kayaks, fishing vessels, sailboats, and cruise ships navigating the nearby waters.

The Porcupine Islands and Frenchman Bay as seen from the summit of Champlain Mountain

On the return trip, take care descending from the summit; missteps on down-sloping rocks can result in falls. The rocks are particularly hazardous when wet. Keep a camera handy below Huguenot Head to capture glorious views of The Tarn from the cliffs above.

An alternative to the out-and-back hike is a traverse of Champlain Mountain and The Beehive, an unmistakably precipitous peak directly south of the Champlain Mountain ridge. To set up a shuttle for this option from the Beachcroft Trailhead parking area, return 0.3 miles on ME 3 to the Park Loop Road, a one-way drive traveling east. Enter Acadia National Park and pass through a tollgate, where a day-use fee or a National Park Pass is required. Drive 3 miles on the Park Loop Road to a parking area on the left across the road from Beehive Trailhead. Allow at least an additional hour to complete the traverse, plus time necessary to run the shuttle.

To complete the traverse from the summit of Champlain Mountain, hike south along the Champlain Mountain ridge on totally exposed Bear Brook Trail. Views to the south and east from the ridge are continuous and outstanding. Descend first gradually and then more steadily to a beautiful mountain pond called The Bowl at 1.1 miles. Skirt the southwest shore of The Bowl and reach Beehive Trail on the left at 1.2 miles. Climb quite steeply to the summit of The

Beehive at 1.5 miles and enjoy its excellent views of the southeast coastline of Mount Desert Island and Penobscot Bay. Drop down abruptly from the summit, using iron-rung ladders in a couple of spots, to a trail junction on the right at 1.6 miles. This junction connects with Gorham Mountain Trail. Hike an additional 0.2 miles to the trailhead at 1.79 miles.

Two additional hiking options are available on Champlain Mountain. Precipice Trail climbs very steeply from the Park Loop Road 1.5 miles north of The Beehive Trailhead. Climbers should be prepared for a narrow path with high, vertical drops and iron-rung ladders that scale sections of perpendicular cliff. This is not a trail for those afraid of heights. Contact Park Headquarters prior to a planned hike on Precipice Trail to ensure it is open. It is not recommended when the trail is wet or icy. The second option is the northern portion of Bear Brook Trail, which ascends to the summit from a trailhead 1 mile north of Precipice Trail on the Park Loop Road. Although not as steep as Precipice Trail, it is fully exposed and climbs steadily on a boulder-strewn path for slightly more than a mile.

History, Weather, and Lodging

Champlain Mountain is named for the French explorer Samuel de Champlain, who sailed the coastal waters of Mount Desert Island in 1604. He was particularly impressed with the treeless, granite summits of Champlain Mountain and the other peaks on the island and named it *Isle des Monts Desert,* or the Island of Barren Mountains.

Peregrine falcons build their nests on the sheer cliffs of the east face of Champlain Mountain. These endangered raptors can fly at speeds in excess of 200 miles per hour when hunting and are protected under the Maine Endangered Species Act. Park officials have concluded that nesting falcons are vulnerable to human disturbances, so nearby trails are closed for several months each year.

The exposed trails and summit of Champlain Mountain are subject to sun, rain, cold, and wind. Harsh onshore winds frequently gather in the Gulf of Maine and unleash gales on the mountain. Fog and coastal showers are also common occurrences. Obtain a reliable mountain forecast before beginning a climb and carry appropriate protective clothing. Spring, summer, and fall are all good seasons to hike Champlain Mountain.

Numerous resorts, hotels, motels, and bed-and-breakfasts are available on Mount Desert Island. Acadia National Park operates the Blackwoods Campground south on ME 3, and several private campgrounds are scattered around the island. Bar Harbor is a well-known shopping destination, and several retailers cater to hikers and climbers.

07 *Cadillac Mountain*
GORGE PATH AND NORTH RIDGE TRAIL LOOP

GPS Trailhead Coordinates

UTM Zone (WGS 84)	19T
Easting	0561950
Northing	4913352.1
Latitude	N 44° 22'22.09"
Longitude	W 68° 13'18.95"

𝕂 Key Information

LENGTH 3.78 miles (4.68 miles without shuttle)

ROUTE CONFIGURATION Loop

DIFFICULTY Moderate

ELEVATION GAIN Slightly exceeds 1,300 feet

SCENERY Spectacular views of Penobscot and Frenchman bays and Mount Desert Island

EXPOSURE Considerable above-tree line exposure to the elements

TRAIL TRAFFIC Heavy

TRAIL SURFACE Rocky throughout

CLIMBING TIME 4 hours

DRIVING DISTANCE 49 miles from Interstate 95 and Interstate 395 in Bangor, ME

ACCESS National Park Pass or park fees required

MAPS USGS Quadrangles for Bar Harbor and Seal Harbor

FACILITIES No trailhead facilities; restrooms, water, and snack bar at the summit

WATER REQUIREMENT 1.5 quarts per person recommended

DOGS ALLOWED Yes

ELEVATION PROFILE

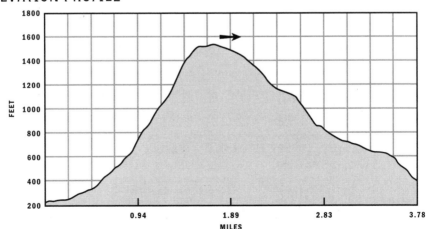

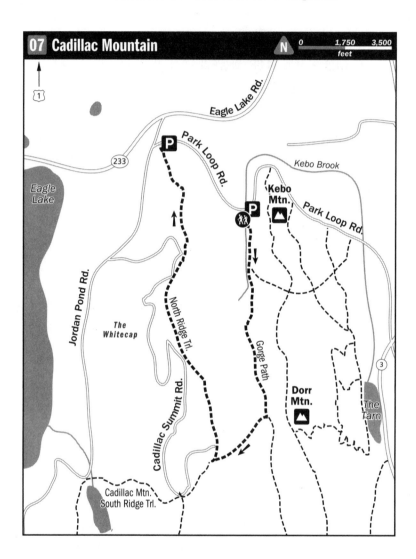

Directions

From the intersection of I-95 and I-395 in Bangor, ME, follow I-395 east 5.2 miles to US 1A in Brewer. Continue east on US 1A 23 miles to the junction with US 1 in Ellsworth. Follow US 1 north 1 mile through the Ellsworth business area to a junction with ME 3. Drive 8.4 miles on ME 3 to ME 102 on Mount Desert Island. Turn right on ME 102 and continue 4.3 miles. Turn left on ME 198 and drive 1.4 miles. Turn left on ME 233 and travel 4.6 miles. Turn right on Jordan Pond Road and enter Acadia National Park. Drive 0.3 miles on Park Loop Road (one-way road) to a

parking area on the left. The ending trailhead for North Ridge Trail is directly across the road. Leave a vehicle here if you're planning for a shuttle. Parking and the beginning trailhead for Gorge Path is on the right 0.9 miles farther on Park Loop Road. The park fee will be collected at a tollgate located 3 miles south on Park Loop Road when you exit the area after the hike.

In Brief

At an elevation of 1,532 feet, Cadillac Mountain is the high point on Mount Desert Island and the tallest mountain along the eastern seaboard of the United States. The colorful history and magnificent beauty of Cadillac Mountain make it one of Maine's most interesting and visited landmarks. Expect rocky hiking conditions throughout and some boulder scrambling, particularly on Gorge Path. Much of the hike is exposed and provides outstanding views of the island and surrounding bays.

Description

Gorge Path is steeper than North Ridge Trail and more difficult to follow when descending from the summit. Further, it parallels and crosses Kebo Brook for the first 0.4 miles and may be impassable during periods of high water. The recommended loop trip is to ascend Gorge Path and return via North Ridge Trail. If Kebo Brook is too high, an out-and-back hike on the stream-free North Ridge Trail is a good option.

From the trailhead, hike in a southerly direction on a narrow trail that skirts Kebo Brook in a lightly forested area. Since it is sheltered from sunlight, this section of trail is often damp and cool even during dry, warm periods. Climb more steadily after 0.3 miles, as the trail narrows and ascends more precipitously past a series of small waterfalls and cataracts. Pass a side trail on the left at 0.4 miles that connects with Kebo Trail to the east. Continue up the rocky, constricted passage to a trail junction in a narrow notch between Cadillac and Dorr mountains at 1.25 miles. Here, Dorr Mountain Trail leaves in an easterly direction and A. Murray Young Trail continues to the south.

From the junction, continue southwesterly on Gorge Path. Emerge above tree line and climb steeply 0.5 miles to the summit. Most of the remainder of the hike will be above tree line with significant exposure to sun, rain, cold, and wind. Onshore winds from Penobscot Bay and the Atlantic Ocean are common, so be prepared for blustery conditions.

Cadillac Mountain dominates Mount Desert Island as it towers majestically above the other 16 granite-covered peaks on the island. From the summit, enjoy breathtaking panoramic vistas of the island and surrounding bays with unmatched views of the glaciated coastal landscape. The Porcupine Islands and Frenchman Bay are to the north, and Dorr and Champlain mountains lie to the east, with Schoodic Point in the distance. Immediately south is Pemetic Mountain, with Seal Harbor and the Cranberry Isles in Penobscot Bay beyond. To the west is Sargent Mountain, with the inland extreme of the Somes Sound fjord just barely visible to its north.

Traffic and crowds somewhat detract from the beauty of the summit. The 3.5-mile Cadillac Summit Road provides access to the top. Besides vehicular traffic, cyclists and occasional runners

Hikers descend from the summit of Cadillac Mountain.

make the ascent, sometimes overpopulating the summit area. There is a visitor center with a snack bar, restrooms, and running water on the south side of the summit parking area.

The trailhead for North Ridge Trail at 1.9 miles is located opposite the visitor center on the north side of the parking area. Descend steadily north on the granite slabs of this exposed trail that faces beautiful Frenchman Bay—it seems to look almost directly down into the streets of Bar Harbor. Follow cairns and blue blazes as the rock- and boulder-strewn trail weaves along to the east of the auto road and continues to drop unfalteringly through mountain scrub. At mile 2.4 and again at mile 3.1, the trail almost connects with the auto road. Take a few final glimpses of picturesque Frenchman Bay before entering a conifer forest just before reaching the Loop Road at mile 3.78. Walk easily for 0.9 miles on the Loop Road to the beginning trailhead.

Five major hiking trails lead to the summit of Cadillac Mountain. In addition to North Ridge Trail and Gorge Path, Dorr Mountain Trail approaches from the east, Cadillac West Trail from the west, and South Ridge Trail from the south. Numerous other trails connect with these. In all, there are more than 120 miles of trails in Acadia National Park.

History, Weather, and Lodging

In prehistoric times, Mount Desert Island was inhabited by Native Americans who lived along its shores at least 5,000 years ago and subsisted by fishing, clamming, and hunting sea mammals. When the first European explorers arrived, the Wabanaki Native Americans, known as the People of the Dawn, were living there. Italian mariner John Cabot, in the service of England, probably sailed along the island in 1497. The first reliable record of European contact was by French explorer Samuel Champlain in 1604. He named the island *Isle des Monts Desert,* or the Island of Barren Mountains. In 1918, Cadillac Mountain was named for another French explorer, Antoine Laumet de La Mothe sieur de Cadillac.

Due to its proximity to the ocean, the weather on Cadillac Mountain can change quickly and become severe. High winds are often a problem, and the Penobscot Bay region is notorious for foggy conditions. Prior to climbing, obtain a reliable mountain weather forecast. The best time for a hike on Cadillac Mountain is summer and early fall.

Mount Desert Island and Acadia National Park are popular destinations for outdoor enthusiasts. Scores of resorts, hotels, motels, and bed-and-breakfasts can be found in the many towns and villages scattered around the island. Numerous private campgrounds dot the area, and Acadia National Park operates Blackwoods Campground a few miles south of Cadillac Mountain on ME 3. Several outfitting retailers operate businesses that cater to hikers and climbers in Bar Harbor and nearby Ellsworth.

08 *Parkman and Bald Mountains*
PARKMAN, BALD, AND HADLOCK BROOK TRAILS LOOP

GPS Trailhead Coordinates

UTM Zone (WGS 84)	19T
Easting	0556480.5
Northing	490802.4
Latitude	N 44° 19'32.92"
Longitude	W 68° 17'28.13"

🚶 Key Information

LENGTH 2.15 miles

ROUTE CONFIGURATION Loop

DIFFICULTY Easy

ELEVATION GAIN Slightly exceeds 800 feet

SCENERY Outstanding views of Mount Desert Island, Penobscot Bay, and Somes Sound Fjord

EXPOSURE Considerable above–tree line exposure to the elements

TRAIL TRAFFIC Moderate to heavy

TRAIL SURFACE Dirt and granite ledges

CLIMBING TIME 2 hours

DRIVING DISTANCE 46.1 miles from Interstates 95 and 395 in Bangor, ME

ACCESS No fees or permits required

MAPS USGS Quadrangle for Southwest Harbor

FACILITIES None

WATER REQUIREMENT 1 quart per person recommended

DOGS ALLOWED Yes

ELEVATION PROFILE

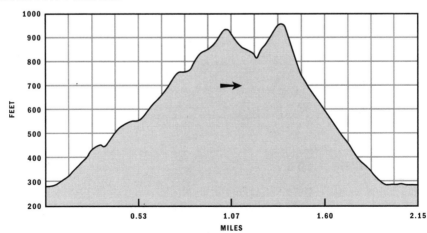

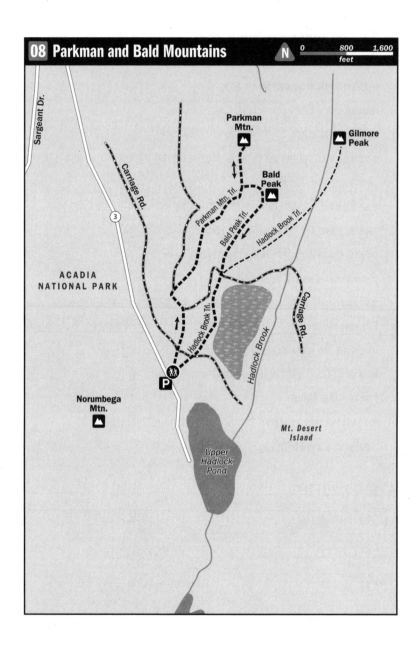

Directions

From the intersection of I-95 and I-395 in Bangor, ME, follow I-395 east 5.2 miles to US 1A in Brewer. Continue east on US 1A 23 miles to the junction with US 1 in Ellsworth. Follow US 1 north 1 mile through the Ellsworth business district to the junction with ME 3. Drive straight

on ME 3 8.4 miles to ME 102 on Mount Desert Island. Turn right on ME 102 and continue 4.3 miles. Turn left on ME 198 and go 4.2 miles to a parking area on the right. The trailhead is across ME 198, up the road 100 feet, and marked with a wooden sign.

In Brief

The Parkman and Bald mountains loop trip is an easy hike in the heart of Acadia National Park on Mount Desert Island. Both peaks are slightly below 1,000 feet in elevation and have some exposure to sun, wind, cold, and rain. You'll hike a wide variety of terrain here, including dirt, boulder-strewn, and granite-slab trail, with some rock scrambling on ledges partway up Parkman Mountain.

Description

From the parking area, carefully cross busy ME 198 and walk back up the road 100 feet to the trailhead, marked with a wooden sign. Enter a dense predominantly conifer forest on Hadlock Brook Trail and go 50 yards to Parkman Mountain Trail on the left. This is the beginning and ending point for the recommended loop trip. I advise you to start on Parkman Mountain Trail, as two near-vertical ledges are more easily negotiated when ascending this trail.

Cross the famous Acadia National Park Carriage Road three times in the next 0.3 miles. Be alert for speeding cyclists and occasional equestrians while traversing the gravel road. At 0.4 miles watch for blue blazes identifying the correct route and scramble up two short, precipitous ledges. Emerge above tree line and follow cairns and blazes on a steady incline over huge granite slabs to the trail junction with Bald Peak Trail at 0.9 miles. Turn left at the junction and climb over steep, rocky terrain on Parkman Mountain Trail for 0.15 miles to the summit marked with a wooden sign and a large cairn.

From the summit of barren Parkman Mountain, you'll enjoy excellent views of Somes Sound Fjord in the west. Carved by glaciers thousands of years ago, the 7-mile-long body of water is reputed to be the only fjord on the East Coast of the United States. It's a popular destination for sea kayakers, and hikers can often observe them navigating the sound's protected waters. The summit is also the beginning of Grandgent Trail, which traverses east over Gilmore Peak to the summit of Sargent Mountain.

Return on the Parkman Mountain Trail 0.15 miles to the Bald Peak Trail junction in the col between Parkman Mountain and Bald Peak. Hike through scrub and then climb the steep path to the summit cairn on exposed Bald Peak at 1.3 miles. This vantage point provides a panoramic vista of the surrounding area with Sargent and Penobscot mountains towering in the east and Norumbega Mountain to the immediate west. To the south, take in Upper and Lower Hadlock Ponds, Northeast Harbor, and Cranberry Isles in beautiful Penobscot Bay.

Depart the summit and descend steadily down the sloping granite ledge on the open southwest face; this descent affords continuous views to the south. Enter a mixed conifer and hardwood forest and cross Carriage Road at 1.7 miles. Here the trail is a combination of loose rocks, dirt, and exposed tree roots. Expect wet conditions for the rest of the trip, as numerous mountain

streams are in the area. At 1.8 miles join and follow Hadlock Brook Trail west and cross over Carriage Road a second time. Pass the trail junction for Parkman Mountain Trail on the right at 2.1 miles and walk the remaining 50 yards to ME 198.

Several excellent hikes are available in the Parkman and Bald mountains region. From the parking area, Norumbega Mountain Trail climbs steeply to the summit with outstanding views of the entire Somes Sound Fjord. Either a short out-and-back hike or a longer loop trip is possible. The Grandgent and Hadlock Brook trails both provide much longer hikes that afford access to the summits of Penobscot and Sargent mountains.

History, Weather, and Lodging

Acadia National Park enjoys a long and varied history of hiking in the mountains. Native Americans used paths for hunting and traveling in prehistoric times. Early European settlers built trails for logging and to connect villages. In the 19th century, Mount Desert Island attracted wealthy urbanites, known as rusticators, with its rugged beauty and quiet, peaceful environment. Many of the rusticators were avid hikers who were responsible for building several of the present-day trails.

In the 1930s, Civilian Conservation Corp (CCC) crews restored and built trails throughout the park. The result is the most extensive trail system in the State of Maine. Today, more than 120 miles of well-maintained trails in Acadia National Park ascend and traverse virtually every peak on the island.

The carriage roads of Acadia National Park provide perhaps the best and most beautiful bike or horse rides in the State of Maine. Walkers and runners also frequent them. Oil magnate John D. Rockefeller Jr. designed and had the carriage roads built over a 27-year period beginning in 1913. Since he was an avid horseman, they were originally intended for horse and carriage. According to park literature, the carriage roads are broken-stone roads, which was a common style at the beginning of the 20th century. These roads are reputedly the best remaining examples of such construction in America. Rockefeller, who contributed substantially to the formation of Acadia National Park, subsequently donated the carriage roads to it.

The higher elevations of the Parkman and Bald mountains loop trip are above tree line and exposed to sun, rain, cold, and wind. However, shelter below tree line is never more than a few minutes away. Carry sufficient protective clothing to address brief periods of exposure to the elements. Summer and fall are the best times to hike Parkman and Bald mountains. Avoid Hadlock Brook and lower Bald Mountain trails during spring or after periods of heavy rain, as nearby streams may flood the paths. An out-and-back hike on Parkman Mountain Trail is a good alternative when these trails are impassable.

Resorts, hotels, motels, and bed-and-breakfasts are available in nearby Northeast and Southwest Harbors, and in most of the towns on Mount Desert Island. Acadia National Park operates Blackwoods Campground, located 6 miles east of the trailhead on ME 3, and numerous private campgrounds dot the island. Several retailers cater to hikers in nearby Bar Harbor and Ellsworth.

A hiker performs yoga near the summit of Parkman Mountain.

09   *Mount Katahdin:* Baxter Peak
HUNT TRAIL

GPS Trailhead Coordinates

UTM Zone (WGS 84)	19T
Easting	0500215.5
Northing	5081299.3
Latitude	N 45° 53'14.22"
Longitude	W 68° 59'48.15"

⚥ Key Information

LENGTH 9.26 miles

ROUTE CONFIGURATION Out-and-back

DIFFICULTY Moderately difficult

ELEVATION GAIN Exceeds 4,150 feet

SCENERY Extended above–tree line views of northwestern Maine and the Katahdin Range

EXPOSURE Considerable above–tree line exposure to the elements

TRAIL TRAFFIC Moderate to heavy

TRAIL SURFACE Dirt and rock below tree line; rocky, boulder-strewn, alpine terrain above

CLIMBING TIME 10 hours

DRIVING DISTANCE 36.5 miles from the junction of Interstate 95 and ME 157 in Medway, ME

ACCESS Day-use or camping fees required

MAPS USGS Quadrangles for Doubletop Mountain and Mount Katahdin

FACILITIES Primitive toilets at the trailhead

WATER REQUIREMENT 2 quarts per person recommended

DOGS ALLOWED No pets allowed in Baxter State Park

ELEVATION PROFILE

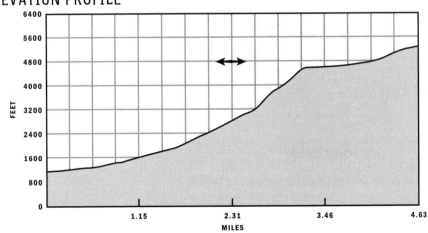

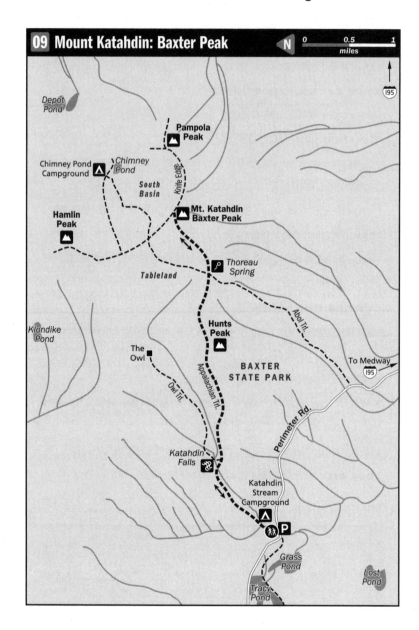

09 Mount Katahdin: Baxter Peak

N   0   0.5   1
miles

195

Depot Pond

Pampola Peak

Chimney Pond Campground

Chimney Pond

Knife Edge

South Basin

Mt. Katahdin Baxter Peak

Hamlin Peak

Thoreau Spring

Tableland

Klondike Pond

The Owl

Hunts Peak

Abol Trl.

To Medway
195

BAXTER STATE PARK

Owl Trl.

Appalachian Trl.

Katahdin Falls

Perimeter Rd.

Katahdin Stream Campground

P

Grass Pond

Lost Pond

Tracy Pond

Directions

From the intersection of I-95 and ME 157 in Medway, ME, follow ME 157 west 1 mile and join ME 11. Follow ME 11 and ME 157 west 10.4 miles through East Millinocket to Central Street in Millinocket. (Watch for spectacular views of the Katahdin massif to the northwest about 3 miles

west of East Millinocket.) Go straight on Central Street 0.2 miles to Katahdin Avenue. Continue straight on Katahdin Avenue 0.2 miles. Turn left on Bates Street and drive 1.5 miles. Turn left on Millinocket Road and drive 5.5 miles to Baxter Park Road. Stay right and follow Baxter Park Road 10 miles to the park gatehouse. Pass through the gate and turn left on the Perimeter Road. Drive 7.7 miles on this good gravel road to Katahdin Stream Campground, with parking, camping, and primitive toilets. The trailhead is located at the northeastern end of the campground.

In Brief

Located in Baxter State Park, historic and legendary Mount Katahdin is the tallest mountain in Maine, at an elevation of 5,267 feet. An out-and-back hike on the Hunt Trail to the summit of Baxter Peak, the northern terminus of the Appalachian Trail, is a moderately difficult climb with considerable exposure to sun, wind, rain, and cold.

Description

Significant boulder-scrambling is required on this rugged alpine path. Severe weather can be a risk, even in the summer months. All the elements that make Mount Washington a difficult and challenging hike are present on Mount Katahdin, but in a more remote setting. Trails are clearly marked and well maintained by park employees.

From the Hunt Trailhead in Katahdin Stream Campground, hike easily on a gentle grade through a thick, predominantly conifer forest for 0.5 miles. The Hunt Trail ascends more steadily to the junction with the Owl Trail on the left at 1.3 miles and closely parallels Katahdin Stream for the first 1.5 miles. Cross Katahdin Stream and hike past a spur trail on the left that leads to Katahdin Stream Falls at 1.4 miles. Take this interesting side hike on your return trip.

The trail continues more steeply on a twisting, rocky path through dense spruce growth for an additional 0.6 miles to a large boulder field. You'll emerge above tree line and scramble over and around huge boulders, carefully following cairns and white blazes for 0.5 miles. Climb even more precipitously and arrive at an alpine plateau called the Tableland at 3.2 miles. The Tableland and summit areas afford unsurpassed views of the lakes and mountains of northwestern Maine. From the Tableland to the summit and back expect continuous exposure to sun, wind, rain, and cold. Carry adequate protection for each of these eventualities during any season. Be alert for thick fog and clouds, which can be disorienting and cause hikers to lose the trail. If weather conditions are untenable, turn back. No good alternatives for shelter from the elements or a quick descent below tree line are available beyond this point.

Follow cairns and blazes and walk easily across the Tableland to Thoreau Spring at 3.7 miles. Water is usually available here but must be treated or purified. The spring is named for author, poet, and philosopher Henry David Thoreau, believed to have arrived at this spot in the summer of 1846 during his explorations of the region. Here, the Abol Trail joins from the southwest after ascending a steep, rocky slide, and Baxter Peak Cut-off Trail leaves to the northeast, circumvents the summit, and connects with the Saddle Trail north of Baxter Peak.

Continue east on the Hunt Trail and gradually traverse the Tableland. After 0.5 miles, climb more steeply over a rocky, boulder-strewn path to the summit, marked with a giant cairn at 4.63

From the summit, father and son look toward Knife Edge.

miles. Baxter Peak provides perhaps the most extensive and breathtaking 360-degree views in the northeastern United States. Directly below in the South Basin is beautiful and serene Chimney Pond. To the east is majestic and intimidating Knife Edge, with barren Pamola Peak standing guard on the far eastern end. Gigantic granite rocks, the Cathedrals, buttress the north wall of South Basin, and beyond is rounded Hamlin Peak with Hamlin Ridge descending east. Trails lead north, south, and east from the summit. Additional trail exploration is not recommended in conjunction with this hike because significant time and energy are required for the return trip. Except in ideal conditions, avoid Knife Edge, as it is a narrow, jagged-rock ridge with sheer cliffs.

Return via the Hunt Trail and descend to Thoreau Spring. Cross the Tableland, drop carefully through the boulder field, and hike to the trail junction for Katahdin Stream Falls. If time permits, take this opportunity to investigate the impressive and picturesque falls, a short hike to the north. The Katahdin Stream Falls trail junction is 1.4 miles from the trailhead.

Several additional hikes are available in the Katahdin Stream Campground region of Baxter State Park: The Owl, elevation 3,736 feet, is a little more than 2 miles from the junction with Hunt Trail near Katahdin Stream Falls. Two miles south of Katahdin Stream Campground on

Perimeter Road, Abol Trail ascends steeply to Thoreau Spring from Abol Campground. The trailhead for Mount OJI is 2.6 miles farther north on the Perimeter Road—a 3-mile hike to a 3,434-foot summit.

History, Weather, and Lodging

Mount Katahdin is rich in history and legend. Native Americans believed the powerful spirit Pamola and other gods dwelt in the hidden reaches of its mysterious summits. The mountain was a sacred place for the tribes of the region; they probably avoided the higher elevations for spiritual reasons. The name, *Katahdin,* is believed to be derived from the Native American word for great or preeminent mountain.

The first recorded ascent was by a group led by Charles Turner, a surveyor from Duxbury, MA, in 1804. Although his account is unclear, they may have taken a route close to the present-day Hunt Trail. Numerous expeditions followed in subsequent decades as logging operations in the area made access easier. The most famous climb was unsuccessful when Thoreau failed to reach the summit in 1846. Although versions differ, he apparently ascended the mountain somewhere near the Abol Slide and didn't quite reach the top. In 1864, he published a book, *The Maine Woods,* which chronicles his climb on Katahdin and his adventures in northern Maine over an 11-year period.

The northern terminus of the Appalachian Trail (AT) is on Mount Katahdin in Baxter State Park. The AT is a continuous 2,160-mile footpath that begins on Springer Mountain in Georgia and ends with a 4.6-mile hike on the Hunt Trail to Baxter Peak. To obtain information about camping reservations or access to Baxter State Park, visit their Web site at www.baxter stateparkauthority.com or call (207) 723-5140. Make reservations early, as there is a high demand for campsites. Day-trippers from outside the park should arrive at the gate early, as park authorities limit the number of vehicles at parking areas.

Severe weather can occur on Mount Katahdin during any season of the year. Obtain a reliable weather forecast at least a week in advance of a planned climb and then consult park officials on the day of the hike. Normally, a summit forecast can be obtained at the ranger's cabin at Katahdin Stream Campground. Park officials close trails when they determine potentially dangerous conditions exist. Carry adequate protective clothing and equipment to withstand considerable exposure to the elements. Potentially cold spring and fall temperatures make summer the best time for a hike on Mount Katahdin. The park is officially closed for most activities prior to May 15th and after October 15th. Special rules apply, and permission is required for winter hiking and climbing.

Mount Katahdin is located in a remote area with limited lodging accommodations. A few motels, hotels, and bed-and-breakfasts can be found in nearby Millinocket, East Millinocket, and Medway. Several private campgrounds are also available, and camping is allowed on a first-come, first-serve basis at Maine Forest Service Campsites in the surrounding area. Usually, the most convenient option for hiking is to reserve a campsite in Baxter State Park.

10   *Mount Katahdin:* Hamlin Peak
CHIMNEY POND AND HAMLIN RIDGE TRAILS

GPS Trailhead Coordinates

UTM Zone (WGS 84)	19T
Easting	0511135.8
Northing	5085334.7
Latitude	N 45° 55'14.08"
Longitude	W 68° 51'21.18"

𝕸 Key Information

LENGTH 8 miles

ROUTE CONFIGURATION Out-and-back

DIFFICULTY Moderately difficult

ELEVATION GAIN Exceeds 3,200 feet

SCENERY Expansive views of North and South basins, Baxter and Pamola peaks, and Knife Edge from Hamlin Ridge and the summit area

EXPOSURE Considerable exposure to the elements

TRAIL TRAFFIC Heavy on Chimney Pond Trail and moderate to light on Hamlin Ridge and above

TRAIL SURFACE Dirt and rocky below tree line; boulder-strewn above

CLIMBING TIME 8 hours

DRIVING DISTANCE 36.9 miles from the junction of Interstate 95 and ME 157 in Medway, ME

ACCESS Day-use and camping fees required

MAPS USGS Quadrangles for Katahdin Lake and Mount Katahdin

FACILITIES Primitive toilets at the trailhead

WATER REQUIREMENT 2 quarts per person recommended

DOGS ALLOWED No pets allowed in Baxter State Park

ELEVATION PROFILE

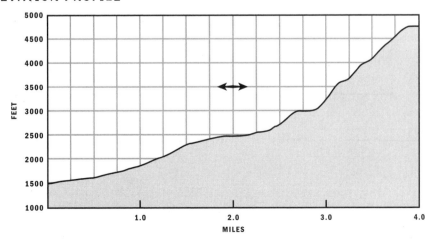

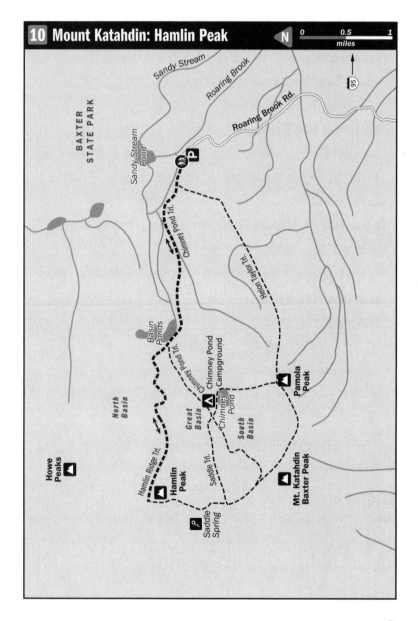

10 Mount Katahdin: Hamlin Peak

N

0   0.5   1
miles

Sandy Stream

Roaring Brook

Roaring Brook Rd.

95

BAXTER STATE PARK

Sandy Stream Pond

P

Chimney Pond Trl.

Helon Taylor Trl.

Basin Ponds

Chimney Pond Trl.

Chimney Pond Campground

Pamola Peak

North Basin

Great Basin

Chimney Pond

South Basin

Howe Peaks

Hamlin Ridge Trl.

Hamlin Peak

Saddle Trl.

Mt. Katahdin Baxter Peak

Saddle Spring

Directions

From the intersection of I-95 and ME 157 in Medway, ME, follow ME 157 west 1 mile and join ME 11. Follow ME 11 and ME 157 west 10.4 miles through East Millinocket to Central Street in Millinocket. Watch for spectacular views of the Katahdin massif to the northwest about 3 miles west of East Millinocket. Go straight on Central Street 0.2 miles to Katahdin Avenue. Continue straight on Katahdin Avenue 0.2 miles. Turn left on Bates Street and drive 1.5 miles. Turn left on Millinocket Road and continue 5.5 miles to Baxter Park Road. Stay right and follow Baxter Park Road 10 miles to the park gatehouse. Pass through the gate and drive straight 8.1 miles on a good gravel road to Roaring Brook Campground, where you'll find parking, camping, and primitive toilets. The Chimney Pond trailhead is located on the far northern end of the parking area just to the right of the ranger's cabin.

In Brief

At an elevation of 4,756 feet, Hamlin Peak is the second-highest true summit on the Katahdin massif. This hike is perhaps the best-kept secret in Baxter State Park. While Baxter Peak regularly attracts heavy hiking traffic, numbers are generally low on magnificent Hamlin Ridge. A ridge between two cirques, it provides exceptional views of Chimney Pond, North and South basins, Baxter and Pamola peaks, and Knife Edge. Trails are clearly marked and in very good condition.

Description

From the trailhead, hike easily on the wide, gradual Chimney Pond Trail along aptly named Roaring Brook for 0.3 miles to the Helon Taylor Trail junction on the left. Continue hiking on a gentle grade along the brook for 0.6 miles before crossing the south branch of Roaring Brook, which flows from Pamola Pond. Begin climbing more steadily on a well-defined path through a mixed hardwood and evergreen forest and then level off at 1.8 miles. Reach the pristine Lower Basin Pond in 0.1 mile with its splendid views of Hamlin Ridge and Mount Katahdin. Watch for moose anywhere in Baxter State Park but particularly in the Chimney Pond Trail area.

Follow a rocky trail around the south shore of Lower Basin Pond for 0.2 miles to the North Basin Cut-off Trail junction on the right at 2.1 miles. Turn right and hike a narrow trail through a thick spruce forest, first gradually and then steeply, for 0.6 miles to North Basin Trail. Go left 0.2 miles on a flat section of cramped path to Hamlin Ridge Trail on the right at 2.9 miles.

Initially, Hamlin Ridge Trail climbs steeply through dense, stunted evergreen growth. After 200 yards, you will emerge above tree line and continue up steadily over a huge, sloping granite ledge. Once above tree line, expect continuous exposure to sun, rain, cold, and wind on the trip to the summit and back. High winds frequently gust over the ridge, which is totally exposed on both the north and the south. Carry adequate protective clothing and gear during any season.

Ascend west up the ragged, boulder-strewn spine of the ridge, while experiencing the phenomenal views it provides. Remote, rarely visited North Basin is below on the north side of the ridge with the Howe Peaks towering beyond. To the south is Chimney Pond in the South Basin cirque, almost completely enveloped in cliffs with Baxter Peak, Knife Edge, and Pamola Peak peering down ominously. Follow cairns and blazes while scrambling over and around huge boulders and rock formations on the ridge until the trail turns slightly north and the gradient diminishes at 3.9 miles. Edge along the top of the cliffs on the west face of North Basin and arrive at the slightly rounded summit of Hamlin Peak, marked with a large cairn at just over 4 miles.

Because the summit area of Hamlin Peak is rounded, it does not provide the dramatic views witnessed from the ridge. However, when clear, Baxter Peak is visible to the south and the Howe Peaks to the north. Hikers can also appreciate the enormity of the massif when studying the expansive plateaus to the northwest and southwest. Hamlin Peak is also the southern terminus of North Peaks Trail, which climbs and traverses the Howe Peaks from the north. Allot at least four hours of daylight for the return trip and descend carefully, particularly on the ridge, where loose rocks make footing tenuous.

If sufficient time and weather conditions permit, an alternative loop trip from the summit of Hamlin Peak to Chimney Pond is an option. The loop adds 1 mile and approximately an hour of hiking time to the trip. It should not be attempted unless all participants have the extra energy and stamina required. If any signs of stormy weather or impending cloud cover exist, avoid this option, as it has extended high-elevation exposure to the elements.

To complete the loop, leave Hamlin Peak and continue west on Hamlin Ridge Trail, dropping down over large rocks for 0.2 miles to Caribou Spring, where there is a large cairn and trail sign. Water is usually available here but must be treated or purified, as should all water in Baxter State Park. Hamlin Ridge Trail joins Northwest Basin Trail at this juncture. Turn left and head almost due south toward Baxter Peak on a gradual down-sloping grade over a boulder field for 0.5 miles. Arrive near a precipice on the left arising from the northwest corner of South Basin. This relatively flat, low area between Baxter and Hamlin peaks is called the Saddle. Walk easily for 0.3 miles to the Saddle Trail junction.

Saddle Trail continues south to Baxter Peak or east to South Basin. Turn left (east) and drop abruptly for 0.4 miles on a steep rock-and-gravel trail toward Chimney Pond. Step carefully to avoid slipping on loose rocks in this area. Arrive at tree line and hike through a sparse evergreen forest for 0.6 miles to Chimney Pond Campground, where there is a Ranger Cabin, primitive toilets, and water. Have your camera available to capture the panoramic vista of Pamola Peak, Knife Edge, Baxter Peak, and the Cathedral Rocks from the northeast shore of Chimney Pond. Be alert for moose that frequent the area. The only access to Chimney Pond Campground is via hiking trails, and it is a popular destination for backpackers. Reservations are required at the campground, which has a bunkhouse and several lean-tos.

Leave Chimney Pond Campground and descend east on Chimney Pond Trail 1 mile to the North Basin Cut-off Trail junction on the left. This completes the loop. Continue down Chimney Pond Trail 2.1 miles to the beginning trailhead at Roaring Brook Campground.

Two excellent hikes are available from Roaring Brook Campground. Both begin at the Chimney Pond trailhead. A 2-mile hike goes north to the open summit of 3,122-foot South Turner Mountain via Russell Pond and South Turner Mountain trails. The South Turner Mountain Trail skirts Sandy Stream Pond, where you can often see moose feeding. This summit

affords outstanding views of Mount Katahdin and North and South basins. Another option is to hike Chimney Pond and Helon Taylor trails a little over 3 miles to the summit of Pamola Peak, which is on the eastern end of Knife Edge.

History, Weather, and Lodging

Baxter State Park is the result of the vision and perseverance of one man, former Maine Governor Percival P. Baxter. For more than three decades, beginning in 1930, he purchased and gifted land to the State of Maine for the express purpose of creating a "forever wild" preserve. In 1933, the Maine Legislature officially designated his first purchase of 6,000 acres, which included Mount Katahdin, as Baxter State Park.

By 1962, he had purchased more than 200,000 acres of wilderness area adjacent to Mount Katahdin, which included 46 mountain peaks. Baxter State Park had become a destination for hikers, climbers, naturalists, and outdoor enthusiasts from all over the world. Since then, the State of Maine has acquired and added acreage to the park.

Severe weather is always a risk on Mount Katahdin. When you plan a climb, always obtain a reliable weather forecast several days in advance of your trip. On the day of the hike, obtain a summit forecast at the Roaring Brook Campground ranger's cabin and check to ensure the trails are open. Always carry sufficient clothing and equipment to protect against significant exposure to the elements. In northern Maine, cold weather lingers into late spring and arrives in early September in Baxter State Park. Summer is normally the best time for a climb on Mount Katahdin. The park is officially closed for most activities prior to May 15th and after October 15th.

Mount Katahdin is located in a remote area with limited lodging accommodations. A few motels, hotels, and bed-and-breakfasts can be found in nearby Millinocket, East Millinocket, and Medway. Several private campgrounds are also available, and camping is permitted on a first-come, first-serve basis at Maine Forest Service Campsites in the surrounding area. Usually the best option is to reserve a campsite in Baxter State Park. To obtain information about camping reservations or access to the park, visit their Web site at www.baxterstatepark authority.com or call (207) 723-5140. Demand for campsites is high, so make reservations early. Day users from outside the park should arrive at the gate early, as park authorities limit the number of vehicles at parking areas.

11 *North Traveler Mountain*
NORTH TRAVELER TRAIL

GPS Trailhead Coordinates

UTM Zone (WGS 84)	19T
Easting	0507693.4
Northing	5105825.8
Latitude	N 46° 06'28.76"
Longitude	W 68° 53'59.79"

🚶 Key Information

LENGTH 5 miles

ROUTE CONFIGURATION Out-and-back

DIFFICULTY Moderate

ELEVATION GAIN 2,131 feet

SCENERY Scenic views of South Branch Pond and the Traveler
Mountain Range

EXPOSURE Some exposure to the elements

TRAIL TRAFFIC Light to moderate

TRAIL SURFACE Primarily rock and ledge

CLIMBING TIME 5 hours

DRIVING DISTANCE 43.5 miles from the junction of Interstate 95 and
ME 158 in Sherman

ACCESS Day-use or camping fees required

MAPS USGS Quadrangles for Wassataquoik Lake and The Traveler

FACILITIES Primitive toilets at the trailhead

WATER REQUIREMENT 1.5 quarts per person recommended

DOGS ALLOWED No pets allowed in Baxter State Park

ELEVATION PROFILE

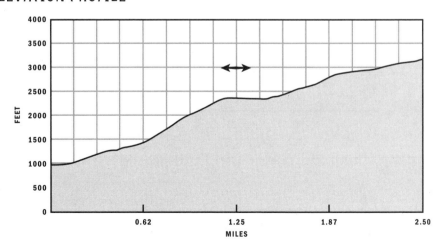

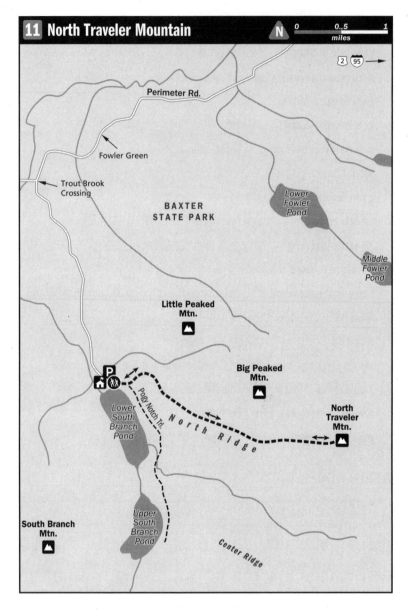

Directions

From the Intersection of I-95 and ME 158 in Sherman, follow ME 158 east 0.5 miles and join ME 11. Turn right on ME 11 and drive north 9.7 miles to the junction with ME 159 on the left in Patten. Drive 8.2 miles on ME 159 to Shin Pond. Continue on Grand Lake Road, a gravel road in good condition, 15.5 miles to the Matagamon Gatehouse in Baxter State Park. After checking in at the gatehouse, follow the Perimeter Road 7.3 miles to Trout Brook Crossing. Turn left onto South Branch Pond Campground Road and go 2.3 miles to the campground. Designated parking areas are adjacent to the campground, and the trailhead is opposite the ranger's cabin on the north shore of South Branch Pond.

In Brief

Located in northern Baxter State Park on the east shore of picturesque South Branch Pond, North Traveler Mountain is one of the more scenic and remote hikes in Maine. Surrounded by mountains, South Branch Pond has the character of an inland fjord. The North Traveler Mountain Trail is moderate in difficulty but provides panoramic views of this unique and beautiful area. The summit elevation is 3,152 feet, and much of the hike is on rock and ledge, with some exposure to sun, rain, wind, and cold. The trail is well marked and in good condition.

Description

From the trailhead adjacent to the ranger's cabin, hike easily in an easterly direction on Pogy Notch Trail along the north shore of South Branch Pond. Several lean-to campsites are located close to the shore between the trail and the pond. These sites provide an excellent base camp for hiking in the South Branch Pond region.

At 0.2 miles, turn left on North Traveler Trail. Climb gradually 0.6 miles in a sparse forest of mixed hardwood and conifer. Begin ascending more steeply at 0.8 miles and arrive at North Ridge Overlook at 1 mile. The overlook is located on the edge of a sheer cliff and faces to the southwest with expansive views of Lower South Branch Pond and South Branch Mountain beyond.

Edge along the cliffs of North Ridge, weaving in and out of stunted evergreen growth while enjoying exceptional views of Peak of the Ridges and The Traveler Mountain to the south. On a clear day, the summits of Mount Katahdin are visible 20 miles farther south. At 1.6 miles, enter and pass through an enchanting stand of white birch, where snowshoe hares abound in the thick undergrowth.

Emerge above tree line and hike gradually, then more steadily over an exposed rock formation slightly above and to the north of the south-face cliffs. At 2.1 miles, reach a gentle grade and enter a thick evergreen growth. After 0.3 miles, leave the forested area and reach the exposed summit marked with a cairn and a sign.

The open summit provides excellent views of the Traveler Range peaks and smaller mountains in northeastern Baxter State Park. Frequently, glimpses of Grand Lake Matagamon can be seen in the north and the East Branch of the Penobscot River in the east.

Hikers near North Ridge Overlook on a fall hike on North Traveler Mountain. In the background, South Branch Pond is beginning to freeze over.

Reenter the forested area and skirt the precipices of the North Ridge on the return trip. Be particularly careful on loose rocks near North Ridge Overlook. The overlook provides a great spot to linger and enjoy a rest or snack before finishing the hike.

A multitude of excellent hikes in the area makes South Branch Campground an outstanding destination for both day-hikers and overnight backpackers. Easy-to-moderate day hikes are available on nearby Center Ridge, Howe Brook, and South Branch Mountain trails. A difficult day hike is a loop that ascends Center Ridge Trail over the summits of Peak of the Ridges, The Traveler, and North Traveler and returns to the campground. This is an arduous climb that should only be attempted by hikers in excellent physical condition with a full day available for hiking. The Pogy Notch Trail leads south into the center of Baxter State Park, where several multiday backpacking opportunities are accessible in the Russell Pond and Wassataquoik Lake areas.

Weather and Lodging

Severe weather can occur in northern Baxter State Park at any time of year. Obtain a reliable weather forecast in advance of a planned trip to the South Branch Pond Campground area. Prior to climbing North Traveler Mountain, get a summit forecast at the ranger's cabin when completing the sign-out register. Park officials close trails when potentially dangerous conditions exist. Cold weather often lasts until late spring and begins in early fall, so the best time for a hike on North Traveler is during the summer. The park is officially closed for most activities from October 15th to May 15th. High winds from the south and west are frequently a factor when hiking the North Traveler Trail. Carry adequate protective clothing and equipment to deal with exposure to the elements.

South Branch Pond and North Traveler Mountain are located in a remote area with very limited lodging accommodations. A couple of small motels are available in nearby Patten, and camping is allowed on a first-come, first-serve basis at a few Maine Forest Service campsites in the surrounding area.

Usually the best option is to reserve a campsite at South Branch Pond Campground in Baxter State Park. To obtain information about camping reservations or access to the park, visit their Web site at www.baxterstateparkauthority.com or call (207) 723-5140. Although the demand for campsites at South Branch Pond is lower than at other campgrounds in the park, making early reservations is recommended. Camping options include 12 lean-tos, 21 tent sites, and an eight-person bunkhouse. Canoeing and sea kayaking are permitted on Upper and Lower South Branch Ponds. Canoe rentals are available at the ranger's cabin.

12　*Bigelow Mountain*
FIRE WARDEN'S TRAIL TO AVERY PEAK

GPS Trailhead Coordinates

UTM Zone (WGS 84)	19T
Easting	0394783
Northing	4995827
Latitude	N 45° 06'36.36"
Longitude	W 70° 20'13.17"

🚶 Key Information

LENGTH 8.76 miles

ROUTE CONFIGURATION Out-and-back

DIFFICULTY Moderately difficult

ELEVATION GAIN Exceeds 2,800 feet

SCENERY Forest hiking with panoramic above–tree line views of Flagstaff Lake and western Maine mountains from the summit

EXPOSURE Above–tree line exposure to the elements east of Bigelow Col

TRAIL TRAFFIC Moderate to light

TRAIL SURFACE Dirt and ledge below Bigelow Col; rocky and boulder-strewn above

CLIMBING TIME 8 hours

DRIVING DISTANCE 79 miles from the junction of Interstate 95 and ME 27 in Augusta, ME

ACCESS No fees or permits required

MAPS USGS Quadrangles for Sugarloaf Mountain and The Horns

FACILITIES Primitive toilets at campsites

WATER REQUIREMENT Two quarts per person recommended

DOGS ALLOWED Yes

ELEVATION PROFILE

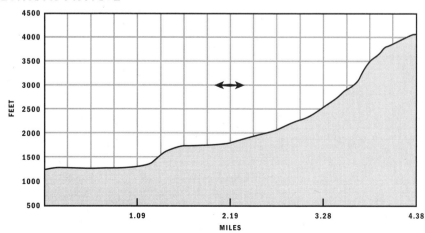

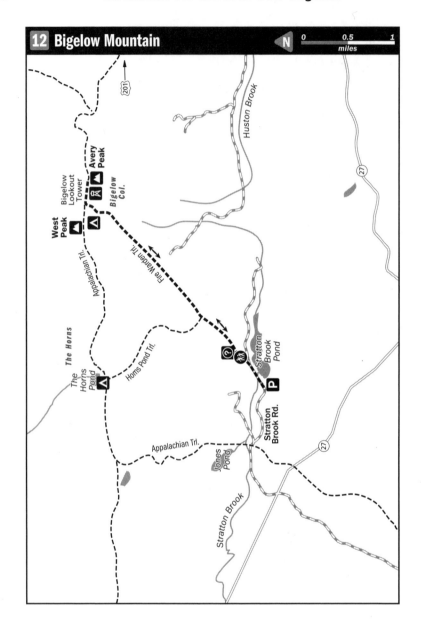

12 Bigelow Mountain

N   0   0.5   1
        miles

Huston Brook

201

Avery Peak

Bigelow Lookout Tower

Bigelow Col.

West Peak

Appalachian Trl.

Fire Warden Trl.

The Horns

The Horns Pond

Horns Pond Trl.

Stratton Brook Pond

P

Stratton Brook Rd.

27

Appalachian Trl.

Jones Pond

Stratton Brook

27

Directions

From the intersection of I-95 and ME 27 in Augusta, ME, follow ME 27 for 67.6 miles through Farmington and Kingfield to the village of Carrabassett Valley. Continue north 9.1 miles to an unmarked dirt road on the right. Travel east on this rough road for 0.9 miles and turn right 150 yards past the junction with the Appalachian Trail. Follow the road for an additional 1.35 miles to where it dead-ends in a parking area. The trailhead is on the east side of the parking area. If conditions are wet, four-wheel or all-wheel-drive vehicles may be necessary, as water tends to pool on the road, creating a muddy surface.

In Brief

Bigelow Mountain, located in the Bigelow Preserve, parallels the south shore of picturesque Flagstaff Lake in the mountains of western Maine. Fire Warden's Trail connects with the Appalachian Trail in Bigelow Col and requires some rock and boulder scrambling in the last 0.3 miles. The summit area offers panoramic views of the mountains and lakes of western Maine.

Description

From the trailhead, hike along the remnants of an old logging road for 0.3 miles to the outlet of Stratton Brook Pond, where an old bridge has been washed out. Rock-hop across Stratton Brook just north of the outlet. *Note:* The brook may be impassable during periods of high water. Follow the road another 0.3 miles to the original trailhead for the Fire Warden's Trail, an abrupt turn to the left. Here, a large wooden bulletin board with a map of the area marks the trail. Be sure to avoid inadvertently continuing on the logging road, which ends in a swampy area several miles to the east.

Hike a gentle grade for 0.6 miles to a moderately steep ledge that gains about 300 feet. Continue on easily to the Horns Pond Trail junction, which begins on the left at 1.6 miles. Be alert for opportunities to spot moose and deer that frequent this area. Leave the junction and ascend more steadily through a conifer and birch forest for 1.9 miles to Moose Falls Tent Site, elevation 2,500 feet. Here, you'll find a primitive toilet, and a source of spring water is nearby. *Note:* All water in the Bigelow Preserve should be treated or purified. From the tent site, the trail climbs quite steeply and unrelentingly for 0.6 miles to the Appalachian Trail junction in Bigelow Col.

Located in a dense evergreen-forested saddle between the two highest peaks in the Bigelow Range, Bigelow Col is home to Myron Avery Campsite, a caretaker's hut and primitive toilet. A spring-fed water supply lies 200 feet down the Fire Warden's Trail on the right. This site is a popular backpacking destination. Several campsites in the Bigelow Preserve provide opportunities for multiday trips into this spectacular wilderness area.

Leave Bigelow Col heading east on the Appalachian Trail and ascend precipitously for 0.3 miles to the summit of Avery Peak. Some rock scrambling is required on this boulder-strewn portion of the trail. Exercise caution in this area, as footing can be dangerous when wet or during stormy weather. The summit is an above–tree line alpine zone with significant exposure to sun, rain, cold, and particularly wind. Gusty winds frequently blow off Flagstaff Lake from the

Tower on summit of Avery Peak

north and sweep across the exposed summits of the Bigelow Range. Be sure to carry wind protection and headgear when climbing above tree line. Follow the cairns and white trail blazes to Bigelow Lookout Tower. Now closed, this structure is all that remains of the former fire tower. The true summit is a few feet to the east and marked by a cairn. The 360-degree views from the summit are truly phenomenal. To the north is expansive Flagstaff Lake, and to the south are Sugarloaf Mountain and the peaks of the Crocker Range. The west is dominated by the slightly higher West Peak, and the elongated summit of Little Bigelow Mountain snakes to the east. Watch for eagles, falcons, osprey, and hawks, which often soar above Flagstaff Lake. Allot at least four hours to ensure a safe descent during daylight.

It is possible to add a partial loop trip to the hike. From Bigelow Col, ascend 0.2 miles west on the Appalachian Trail to the summit of exposed West Peak, elevation 4,150 feet—the high point in the Bigelow Range. Descend steeply and continue on the ridge for 2.1 miles to South Horn. Boulder scrambling is required on this rocky and scrub-covered summit. A boulder-strewn 0.2-mile spur trail to North Horn leaves the main trail just 75 yards west of South Horn and provides a panoramic view of Flagstaff Lake. From South Horn, drop abruptly 0.5 miles to

Horns Pond Campsite, where you'll find a lean-to, several tent sites, and a primitive toilet. Hike .1 mile west from the campsite to the Horns Pond Trail junction and descend gradually for 1.9 miles to the Fire Warden's Trail, 1.6 miles from the beginning trailhead.

Do not consider the loop as an option unless all members of the party are fully prepared to expend substantial additional time and effort. The traverse from Bigelow Col to Horns Pond Campsite adds 800 feet of elevation gain and nearly 3 miles of arduous hiking. Further, there is significant exposure to the elements on West Peak. Assume that hiking the loop will add at least two hours to the length of the trip.

History, Weather, and Lodging

Native Americans inhabited the Bigelow Mountain area for thousands of years. Nearby Dead River, which flowed through what is now Flagstaff Lake, was a major thoroughfare for aboriginal peoples, English and French settlers, and explorers. In 1775, Revolutionary War soldiers under the command of Colonel Benedict Arnold camped in the shadows of Bigelow Mountain on their famous March to Quebec.

Bigelow Mountain was nearly lost as a hiking and wilderness preserve. In the 1970s plans were initiated to develop the mountain as a ski resort. Opponents countered with a statewide referendum, which resulted in the creation of the Bigelow Preserve. Today the entire Bigelow Range is protected from development and managed by the Maine Bureau of Parks and Lands. The preserve consists of more than 36,000 acres of public lands and all seven summits.

Avery Peak was named for pioneer trailblazer Myron Avery, a Maine mountaineering and hiking legend. He founded the Maine Appalachian Trail Club, which maintains the trails in the Bigelow Preserve, and was instrumental in establishing the Appalachian Trail.

The Bigelow Mountain area provides a multitude of additional hiking opportunities. The 2,175-mile Appalachian Trail crosses over nearby Spaulding, Sugarloaf, and Crocker mountains and then traverses most of the Bigelow Range. Bigelow Range Trail leaves from Stratton in the west and travels over the westernmost summit in the range, Cranberry Peak, before joining the Appalachian Trail 2 miles west of Horns Pond Campsite.

The Bigelow Mountain region is notorious for cold atmospheric conditions, and spring snowmelt can cause streams and brooks to be impassable or dangerous. Prior to climbing, obtain a reliable mountain weather forecast. The best time for a hike in the Bigelow region is summer or early fall prior to the arrival of wintry weather conditions.

Bigelow Mountain is located in a remote area with limited lodging choices. However, some lodging is available at Sugarloaf Resort and in the nearby towns of Stratton and Carrabassett Valley. Eustis offers camping 5 miles north of Stratton, and primitive camping is permitted at Maine Forest Service Campsites along the shore of Flagstaff Lake.

13 MOUNT GREYLOCK

MASSACHUSETTS

13 *Mount Greylock*

OLD ADAMS ROAD, CHESHIRE HARBOR, AND APPALACHIAN TRAILS

GPS Trailhead Coordinates

UTM Zone (WGS 84)	18T
Easting	0651100.5
Northing	4719005.5
Latitude	N 42° 36'38.48"
Longitude	W 73° 09'26.72"

👣 Key Information

LENGTH 6 miles

ROUTE CONFIGURATION Out-and-back

DIFFICULTY Moderate

ELEVATION GAIN 1,905 feet

SCENERY Excellent views of the Berkshires of western Massachusetts and the Green Mountains of southern Vermont from the summit

EXPOSURE Minimal exposure to the elements

TRAIL TRAFFIC Moderate to heavy

TRAIL SURFACE Primarily hard-packed dirt and rock

CLIMBING TIME 5 hours

DRIVING DISTANCE Approximately 35 miles from the junction of Interstate 91 and MA 2 in Greenfield, MA

ACCESS No fees or permits required

MAPS USGS Quadrangles for North Adams and Cheshire

FACILITIES None at trailhead; restrooms at the summit

WATER REQUIREMENT 1.5 quarts per person recommended

DOGS ALLOWED Yes

ELEVATION PROFILE

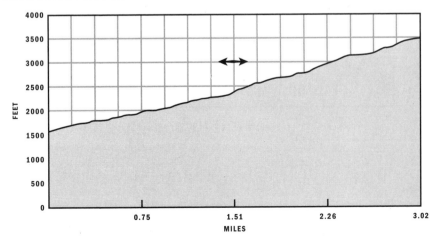

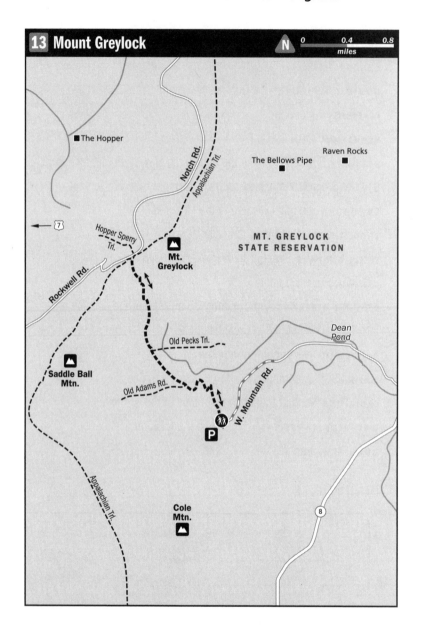

13 Mount Greylock

N

0   0.4   0.8
miles

The Hopper

Notch Rd.

Appalachian Trl.

The Bellows Pipe

Raven Rocks

7

Hopper Sperry Trl.

Rockwell Rd.

Mt. Greylock

MT. GREYLOCK STATE RESERVATION

Old Pecks Trl.

Dean Pond

Saddle Ball Mtn.

Old Adams Rd.

W. Mountain Rd.

P

Appalachian Trl.

Cole Mtn.

8

Directions

From the intersection of I-91 and MA 2 in Greenfield, MA, follow MA 2 west 26.8 miles to MA 8 in North Adams. Drive south on MA 8 4.9 miles to Maple Street on the right in Adams. Go right 0.3 miles to West Street. Turn left and go 0.6 miles on West Street to West Mountain Road on the right. Follow West Mountain Road 1.6 miles to a parking area, where it dead-ends. The last 0.2 miles on West Mountain Road are a good gravel road. The trailhead begins on the right side of the parking area, adjacent to a field.

In Brief

Situated in the picturesque Berkshire Mountains of western Massachusetts, Mount Greylock, elevation 3,491 feet, is the state's highest peak. A hike to the summit via Old Adams Road, Cheshire Harbor, and Appalachian trails is moderate in difficulty, with excellent views from a lookout near the top. The trail surface is predominantly hard-packed dirt and rock, with minimal exposure to the elements.

Description

From the parking area, go right on a dirt road in a small field, past a partially obscured trail sign that is posted on a tree on the left and states "Old Adams Road and Cheshire Harbor Trails to Top." Follow the old road along the western edge of the field 30 yards to the trailhead beside an information kiosk.

Walk 20 yards past a steel gate and ascend Old Adams Road Trail on a wide, hard-packed dirt path in a hardwood forest. Continue steadily upward on an obvious, well-shaded trail in very good condition. At 0.7 miles, encounter a loose-rock surface while negotiating long switchbacks to a fork in the path at 1 mile. Avoid bearing right, which is marked with a red dot on a tree. Angle left, following the blue trail indicator for 0.1 mile to the junction with Cheshire Harbor Trail. The trailhead is clearly marked with a conspicuous sign on the right.

Turn right and persist steadily up the Cheshire Harbor Trail on a loose-rock-and-dirt surface with some trail erosion to gentle, prolonged ledges at 1.2 miles. Continue up the tree root–infested ledges in a heavily eroded section 0.3 miles to Peck's Loop Trail on the right. Recommence climbing steadily, following orange ribbons attached to trees, 0.7 miles to a wide wooden bridge in poor condition. Beyond the bridge, the character of the trail changes to a narrow, constricted hiking route.

Reach the Appalachian Trail, marked with a trail sign, at 2.4 miles. Turn right on the Appalachian Trail. Traverse the paved auto road to a tree sign stating "Summit," with an arrow pointing north, and reenter a wooded area. Hike easily on an attenuated, damp rock path in thick mountain vegetation for 0.15 miles to Hopper Sperry Trail on the left. Continue hiking to a small mountain tarn on the left with a cabin on the opposite shore at 2.6 miles. Follow a boardwalk around the pond for 0.1 mile and cross the auto road at an intersection.

Bascom Lodge, near the summit of Mount Greylock

At 2.7 miles, enter dense spruce growth next to a "Summit" sign and clamber up a precipitous rocky trail under overhanging conifer trees. Emerge on a paved road next to a large stone and concrete barn on the left at 2.9 miles. Primitive toilets are located 100 yards to the right. Follow a sign directing you up the road to the summit and Bascom Lodge and reenter the forest in a tall stand of spruce trees. Go 200 yards and arrive at the preeminent Veterans War Memorial Tower, with Bascom Lodge to the right, at 3 miles.

The Memorial Tower dominates the landscaped summit area. Walk past the high point and down a paved footpath to an overlook facing east. Savor dramatic views of the Town of Adams, the surrounding Berkshire Mountains, and the Green Mountains of Vermont beyond in the north. Return on the Appalachian Trail and descend the Cheshire Harbor and Old Adams Road trails to the parking area in Adams.

Mount Greylock is one of the most popular hikes in Massachusetts, and multiple trails lead to the summit. Thunderbolt and Gould trails ascend the mountain from the east in Adams,

while Hopper Sperry climbs from the west. The Appalachian Trail intersects the summit from south to north, and several side trails join it at varying points.

History, Weather, and Lodging

Situated in Mount Greylock State Reservation, Mount Greylock, elevation 3,491 feet, is the highest point in Massachusetts. The impressive whale-shaped peak dominates the western Massachusetts landscape. Its distinctive shape is reputed to have motivated Herman Melville to write his classic, *Moby-Dick.* Artist Norman Rockwell and philosopher Henry David Thoreau were also attracted to the area for its majestic, inspirational beauty.

Completed in 1932, the Veterans War Memorial Tower is a 100-foot lighthouse-style structure. The tower was constructed to honor the state's dead from World War I. Bascom Lodge offers a dining area, gift shop, restrooms, and lodging. Normally, driving to the summit is possible on the Historic Parkway auto road. However, the road will be closed for renovations until 2009.

Virtually the entire hike to the summit of Mount Greylock is below tree line, with minimal exposure to the elements. When open, Bascom Lodge is a source of shelter from harsh weather. Summer and fall are the best seasons for a climb on Mount Greylock. Autumn treks offer beautiful foliage and less-crowded conditions.

Several communities in the area, including Adams, North Adams, and Pittsfield, offer motels, hotels, and bed-and-breakfasts. Lodging is also an option at Bascom Lodge when it's open. Camping is available in North Adams; campgrounds and backpacker lean-tos are situated at several locations in Mount Greylock State Reservation.

NEW HAMPSHIRE

14   *Mount Lafayette*
           OLD BRIDLE PATH AND GREENLEAF TRAIL

GPS Trailhead Coordinates

UTM Zone (WGS 84)	19T
Easting	0285447.8
Northing	4890941.2
Latitude	N 44° 08'31.89"
Longitude	W 71° 40'54.84"

⛹ Key Information

LENGTH 7 miles

ROUTE CONFIGURATION Out-and-back

DIFFICULTY Moderately difficult

ELEVATION GAIN 3,482 feet

SCENERY Outstanding views of Franconia Ridge and the White Mountains

EXPOSURE Considerable above-tree line exposure to the elements

TRAIL TRAFFIC Moderate to heavy

TRAIL SURFACE Dirt, rock, and ledge below tree line; rocky and boulder-strewn above

CLIMBING TIME 7 hours

DRIVING DISTANCE Approximately 73 miles from the junction of Interstates 93 and 89 in Concord, NH

ACCESS No fees or permits required

MAPS USGS Quadrangle for Franconia

FACILITIES Primitive toilets at the trailhead

WATER REQUIREMENT 2 quarts per person recommended

DOGS ALLOWED Yes

ELEVATION PROFILE

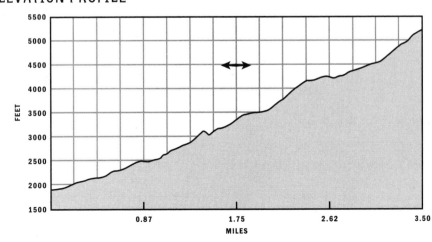

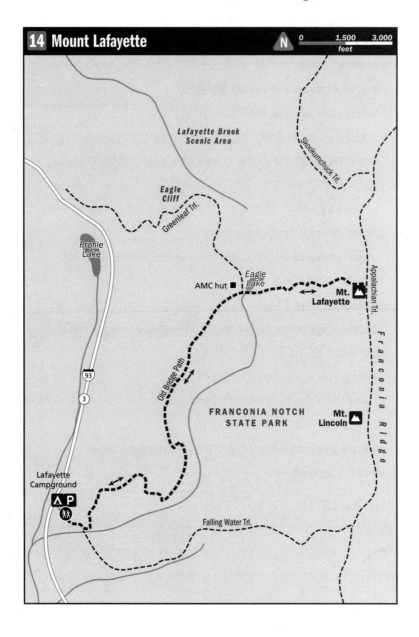

Directions

From the intersection of I-93 and I-89 in Concord, NH, follow I-93 north 72.8 miles and take the exit for the Lafayette Campground. Go 0.1 mile to trailhead parking on the right at Lafayette Place. The trailhead for Old Bridle Path is on the east side of the parking area and passes to the left of an information kiosk and primitive toilets.

In Brief

Named for Revolutionary War hero Marquis de Lafayette, Mount Lafayette, elevation 5,260 feet, is the highest mountain in New Hampshire outside the Presidential Range and the seventh tallest in New England. Located east of Franconia Notch, the summit is on the northern terminus of spectacular Franconia Ridge. Significant rock and boulder scrambling is required, but you will be rewarded at the summit area with unsurpassed 360-degree views of the surrounding White Mountains.

Description

From the trailhead at Lafayette Place, hike easily on Old Bridle Path southeast through a sparse hardwood forest for 0.25 miles to the Falling Waters Trail junction on the right. Turn north on Old Bridle Path and ascend gradually on a hard-packed dirt-and-rock trail. After 1.2 miles, begin to climb more steeply on a boulder-strewn path that rises to a ridge in stunted mountain growth.

Continue to follow the often steep path up the ridge while appreciating sporadic views of imposing Franconia Ridge to the east. Take time to glance back to the west and observe the precipitous cliffs of Cannon Mountain. This was once home to the famous "Old Man of the Mountain," but his granite profile collapsed and fell to the base of the cliffs a few years ago. This seemingly immortal legendary mountain icon is now but a memory.

At 1.6 miles, edge along the cliffs above Walker Ravine and encounter several exposed overlooks. The overlooks provide numerous opportunities to observe the ravine below and Franconia Ridge above. At 2.2 miles, climb steadily through a thickly forested area, then drop into a slight, deadwood-strewn depression. Continue on and arrive at the Appalachian Mountain Club (AMC) Greenleaf Hut at 2.6 miles.

The AMC hut is located at an elevation of 4,200 feet and can accommodate 48 people in two bunkrooms. Water and toilets are available, and some snack food can be purchased. The hut is a popular backpacker destination, particularly for thru-hikers on the Appalachian Trail, which passes over Franconia Ridge less than a mile east. Advance reservations are required at the AMC hut. For more information, access their Web site at www.outdoors.org.

The Old Bridle Path joins Greenleaf Trail at the hut. Follow Greenleaf Trail east, skirt the south shore of an alpine tarn called Eagle Lake at 2.7 miles, and emerge above tree line. From this point, you will encounter continuous exposure to the elements while climbing to and returning from the summit. Severe weather can occur during any season. High winds and cloudy conditions often arise. If stormy weather threatens, descend to the hut or below tree line immediately.

Hikers pause for a view of Mount Lafayette and Franconia Ridge from an overlook on the Old Bridle Path.

Scramble over and around several large rock formations above Eagle Lake for 0.5 miles. Following cairns, hike up a steep granite ledge and huge rock slabs for an additional 0.2 miles and traverse a boulder field to the summit at 3.5 miles. A sign and cairn indicate the top, where Garfield Ridge and Franconia Ridge trails meet.

The summit of Mount Lafayette provides unsurpassed 360-degree views of the New Hampshire White Mountains. To the east are Owl's Head and the Bonds, with Mount Washington and the Presidentials towering beyond. Turning clockwise, narrow, rugged Franconia Ridge extends south over Mount Lincoln and Little Haystack Mountain to Mount Liberty. Due west is stunning Cannon Mountain with the Kinsman Range in the distance. Alpinelike Mount Garfield dominates views to the north. The large rocks that pockmark the summit area provide some shelter from the elements. Take time to feast on the views and a picnic lunch before the return trip. Allow sufficient time for a safe return to Lafayette Place during daylight.

If weather permits, a loop trip encompassing a portion of Franconia Ridge is possible. However, do not consider this option if signs of adverse weather are present. The narrow, totally exposed ridge has a reputation for being dangerous during thunderstorms, and high winds, fog, and clouds can create treacherous conditions. Further, do not attempt the loop trip during periods of high water because of the multiple stream crossings on Falling Waters Trail.

To complete the loop trip, descend gradually south on rocky, boulder-strewn Franconia Ridge Trail. Clamber over a large granite knob and dip to the saddle between Mounts Lafayette

and Lincoln. Climb on a moderate grade to the top of Mount Lincoln at 0.9 miles. With an elevation of 5,089 feet, Mount Lincoln provides exceptional views in all directions.

Drop abruptly on the attenuating ridge to a minor depression and then ascend slightly over a considerable boulder that constitutes the summit of Little Haystack Mountain at 1.5 miles. Just below, on the west side of the summit, is the junction with Falling Waters Trail. Hike down the steep Falling Waters Trail on exposed ledge and enter mountain scrub to a spur trail on the left at 1.9 miles. This short side trail leads to Shining Rock, a remarkable granite ledge that plunges more than 200 feet. Take a few moments to savor its interesting features but avoid the temptation to climb out on the rock face, as it is usually wet and slippery, and falls are always a potential hazard.

Continue to descend via switchbacks on a steep ridge in a dense conifer forest for 0.7 miles. At 2.6 miles, complete the first of several stream crossings. In the next 0.6 miles, pass several impressive waterfalls—the source of the trail name. At 3.5 miles, cross a bridge over Walker Brook and rejoin the Old Bridle Path. Hike easily for 0.25 miles to Lafayette Place.

Franconia Notch is a hiker's paradise. Two miles south of Lafayette Place, trails lead to Mounts Liberty and Flume. To the north, Skookumchuck and Greenleaf trails provide alternate routes to Mount Lafayette. Paths proceed west from Lafayette Place to Cannon and Kinsman mountains and the Lonesome Lake AMC Hut.

History, Weather, and Lodging

Originally named "Great Haystack," Mount Lafayette was renamed for the French military hero Marquis de Lafayette for his invaluable contributions to the Revolutionary War effort. Old Bridle Path is one of several mountain paths that was constructed in the White Mountains during the 19th century specifically for horse traffic. Horses transported mountain visitors to and from a primitive hotel at the summit, where remains of the foundation are still visible.

Adverse and extreme weather are always a risk on Mount Lafayette and Franconia Ridge, so climbers should obtain a reliable weather forecast before their trip. Hikers should always carry protective clothing and gear to address the extraordinary weather variables that can occur in this mountain region. Summer is usually the best time for a climb on Mount Lafayette.

Numerous resorts, hotels, motels, and bed-and-breakfasts are available in nearby Lincoln. The best camping option is Lafayette Campground, adjacent to the trailhead. Also, you can make overnight bunkroom reservations at the Greenleaf AMC Hut. Several retailers in Lincoln cater to hikers and backpackers.

15   *South Moat Mountain*
MOAT MOUNTAIN TRAIL

GPS Trailhead Coordinates

UTM Zone (WGS 84)	19T
Easting	0324864.7
Northing	4873294.9
Latitude	N 43° 59'38.17"
Longitude	W 71° 11'1.10"

🏃 Key Information

LENGTH 5.26 miles

ROUTE CONFIGURATION Out-and-back

DIFFICULTY Easy to moderate

ELEVATION GAIN 2,080 feet

SCENERY Exceptional views of White Mountains of New Hampshire from summit area

EXPOSURE Modest exposure

TRAIL TRAFFIC Moderate

TRAIL SURFACE Dirt, rock, and ledges

CLIMBING TIME 4.5 hours

DRIVING DISTANCE Approximately 80 miles from the junction of Interstate 95 and NH 16 in Portsmouth

ACCESS Day-use parking fee required

MAPS USGS Quadrangles for North Conway West and Silver Lake

FACILITIES None

WATER REQUIREMENT 1.5 quarts per person recommended

DOGS ALLOWED Yes

ELEVATION PROFILE

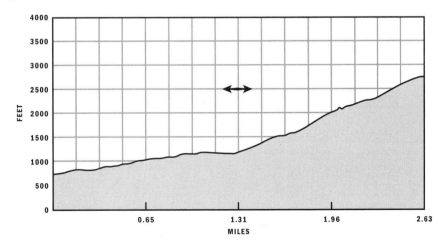

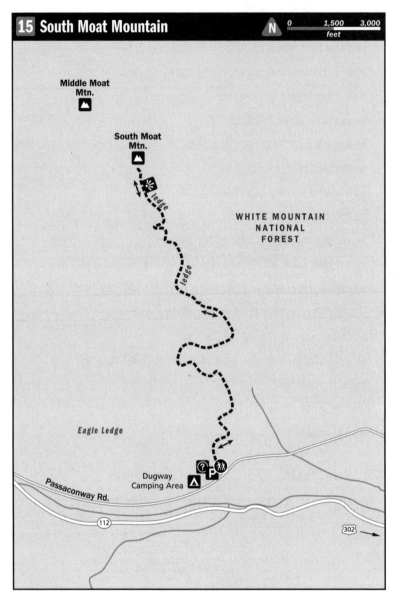

15 South Moat Mountain

N

0   1,500   3,000
feet

Middle Moat
Mtn.

South Moat
Mtn.

ledge

ledge

WHITE MOUNTAIN
NATIONAL
FOREST

Eagle Ledge

Dugway
Camping Area

Passaconway Rd.

112

302

Hikers relax at the summit of South Moat Mountain on a chilly fall day.

Directions

From the intersection of I-95 and NH 16 in Portsmouth, follow NH 16 (which is also NH 4 and Spaulding Turnpike, initially) 75.1 miles to Conway. Turn left on Washington Street and go 0.5 miles to West Side Road. Continue on West Side Road 0.4 miles to Passaconaway Road. Turn left and drive 3.2 miles to a parking area on the right. The trailhead for Moat Mountain Trail leaves from the right rear corner of the parking area, near an information kiosk and self-service pay station.

In Brief

Moat Mountain Trail to the summit of South Moat Mountain, elevation 2,749 feet, is easy to moderate in difficulty, with some ledge scrambling at higher elevations. Located in the heart of the White Mountains, barren Moat Ridge parallels and overshadows North Conway. The ledges

A hiker crosses the bridge over Dry Brook on Moat Mountain Trail.

on the south face and summit area provide exceptional views of the White Mountains in all directions.

Description

From the Moat Mountain trailhead, pass a steel gate and walk easily on a wide, hard-packed dirt path in a mixed deciduous-and-conifer forest. After 50 yards, turn sharply right under an arrow sign posted to a tree on the left. Continue up a gentle gradient, dip down, and cross a small brook at 0.3 miles.

Ascend more steadily in a northwesterly direction for 0.6 miles to an excellent wooden bridge with steel girder support spanning Dry Brook at 1 mile. Recommence easily for 0.3 miles and at 1.3 miles connect with the original Moat Mountain Trail, which is closed below this point. Here the trail surface becomes rockier and the gradient much steeper.

At 1.4 miles, clamber up long, sloping ledges in sparse, stunted mountain vegetation. Climb unrelentingly for 0.3 miles on loose rocks and small boulders and arrive at an open ledge facing south at 1.7 miles. Pause to savor magnificent views of the southern White Mountains.

Carefully follow cairns and yellow blazes in patchy spruce growth for 0.5 miles while negotiating long, often precipitous ledges with sporadic views to the west. At 2.2 miles, emerge above tree line. From here to the summit and back, expect continuous exposure to the elements. Scramble over and around large boulders and oblique ledges on the south shoulder of the mountain for 0.4 miles and arrive at the summit, elevation 2,749 feet, at 2.63 miles.

South Moat Mountain, with a barren, slightly rounded summit, is located in the heart of New Hampshire's White Mountains. If weather permits, plan an extended visit at the top and enjoy outstanding 360-degree views. To the east is picturesque North Conway, with scenic Cranmore Mountain and Ski Area beyond. Just north of Cranmore is Mount Kearsage North, with the distinctive fire tower recognizable on the crest. Moat Ridge extends north over Middle and North Moat Peaks pointing toward the towering Presidential Range. Just east of North Moat, the cliffs of White Horse Ledge, a popular technical climbing area, are visible. The White Mountains dominate the landscape both south and west. Cautiously descend south on the extended ledges and return to the Passaconaway Road trailhead.

A traverse of Moat Ridge is possible but not recommended. This alternative is a rugged hike with poor trail conditions that substantially increase the difficulty of the trek. A multitude of additional climbs are available in the Moat Mountain area. To the north, trails lead over Table, Big Attitash, and Little Attitash mountains. To the south, numerous paths lead to the summit of Mount Chocorua from the Kancamagus Highway and NH 16.

History, Weather, and Lodging

The original Moat Mountain Trail left Passaconaway Road about a mile east of the current trailhead. Due to private-property concerns, the trail was rerouted a couple of years ago. Most maps and guidebooks continue to show the old trailhead as the beginning point for this hike.

South Moat Mountain is located at the southern end of an exposed ridge in the heart of the White Mountains. Gusty northwest winds are a common occurrence, and exposure to sun, rain, and cold should be expected above tree line. Climbers should carry adequate clothing and equipment to address any of these eventualities and obtain a reliable mountain weather forecast prior to a planned trip. Summer and fall are the best times for a hike on South Moat Mountain. Spring should be avoided, as the new section of trail tends to be very muddy after snowmelt and runoff.

Nearby North Conway has a multitude of resorts, hotels, motels, and bed-and-breakfasts. Camping is available at several locations on the Kancamagus Highway and along NH 16 south of Conway. North Conway is a shopping destination, with several retailers that specialize in hiking, mountaineering, and camping equipment and gear.

16   *Mount Kearsarge North*
MOUNT KEARSARGE NORTH TRAIL

GPS Trailhead Coordinates

UTM Zone (WGS 84)	19T
Easting	0331144.6
Northing	4882188.5
Latitude	N 44° 04'31.53"
Longitude	W 71° 06'29.56"

🚶🚶 Key Information

LENGTH 5.6 miles

ROUTE CONFIGURATION Out-and-back

DIFFICULTY Moderate

ELEVATION GAIN 2,583 feet

SCENERY Excellent views of the Presidentials, southern Carter Range, and Evans Notch area from the summit

EXPOSURE Some exposure to the elements

TRAIL TRAFFIC Heavy

TRAIL SURFACE Hard-packed dirt and ledge; some trail erosion

CLIMBING TIME 5 hours

DRIVING DISTANCE Approximately 85 miles from the junction of Interstate 95 and NH 16 in Portsmouth, NH

ACCESS No fees or permits required

MAPS USGS Quadrangle for North Conway East

FACILITIES None

WATER REQUIREMENT 1.5 quarts per person recommended

DOGS ALLOWED Yes

ELEVATION PROFILE

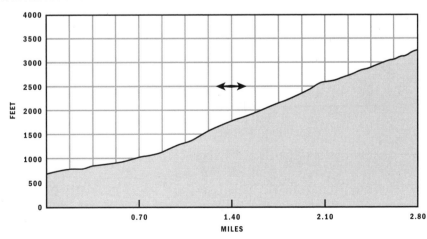

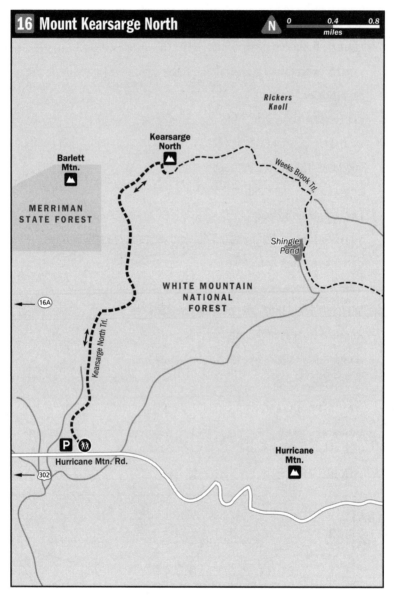

A hiker approaches the fire tower at the summit of Kearsarge North.

Directions

From the intersection of I-95 and NH 16 in Portsmouth, NH, follow NH 16 (which is also NH 4 and the Spaulding Turnpike, initially) 84.3 miles to Hurricane Mountain Road on the right, north of the business district in North Conway. Follow Hurricane Mountain Road 1 mile to a small parking area on the left. The trailhead is marked with a sign and begins to the right of the parking area.

In Brief

Located on the outskirts of North Conway, Kearsarge North, elevation 3,268 feet, is an excellent day hike. Ledges near the summit provide wonderful views of the surrounding mountains, and the historic and distinctive fire tower at the top provides a phenomenal 360-degree outlook.

Hikers descending ledges near summit of Kearsarge North

Description

From the Mount Kearsarge North trailhead, hike easily through a predominantly hardwood forest on a hard-packed dirt trail, formerly an old road. Pass a few homes on the right and continue gradually up the west side of a rounded ridge, paralleling a brook on the left that flows south in a deep ravine below.

At 0.9 miles, some trail erosion diminishes the otherwise high-quality trail conditions. Hike more steadily for 1.1 miles as the gradient increases, and the surrounding forest gradually changes from hardwood to mixed conifer. Open ledges facing west at 2 miles are excellent locations for a rest or snack. Take time to thoroughly savor the views of North Conway, the Saco River Valley, and the barren summits of Moat Mountain beyond.

Carefully proceed up the ledges and enter dense spruce growth on a narrow, shaded path. Continue hiking steadily upward while moving progressively to the northwest over a rounded slope. Rotate slightly to the northeast and scramble up a steep, damp, rocky section of trail at 2.5 miles.

Emerge onto exposed ledges with excellent views to the west and hike circuitously through patchy, stunted mountain growth. Continue ascending the ledges, while catching periodic glimpses of the fire tower commanding the horizon above. Reach the fire tower and the summit at 2.8 miles, where Weeks Brook Trail arrives from the southeast. I do not recommend Weeks Brook Trail, as it is not well marked and is difficult to follow in places.

The fire tower is no longer used by the Forest Service but is open to the public. It provides a great opportunity to find protection from the elements and enjoy sheltered panoramic vistas of the region. Climb the tower stairs and enter the glass-encased enclosure to savor scenic grandeur in all directions. Mount Washington and the Presidentials seem to peer down from the northwest, and the peaks of Evans Notch are due north. Lakes and hills of the western Maine landscape lie to the east, and Mount Cranmore is immediately south. Rugged Moat Mountain dominates the area west of North Conway, with dozens of mountains beyond. The tower is an ideal spot for a leisurely picnic lunch.

On the return trip, descend cautiously down open ledges while enjoying a steady diet of beautiful views to the west and southwest. After reentering and hiking through canopylike spruce growth, take time to linger again on the lower ledges before returning to the parking area.

Several excellent easy-to-moderate hikes are available in the North Conway area. East of town, easy hikes lead to Cranmore and Peaked mountains. North, in Jackson, paths ascend to the summits of Doublehead and Black mountains. Trails lead to Attitash and Moat mountains just west of North Conway.

History, Weather, and Lodging

Like many New Hampshire peaks, the summit of Kearsarge North, originally called Mount Pequawket, was the site of a small hotel in the 19th century. A bridle path was built in 1845 to transport guests by horse. The hotel reputedly "blew off the mountain" and was rebuilt, only to blow away a second time. Eventually, it was replaced in 1909 by one of the early fire towers in New Hampshire. The Forest Service operated the fire tower for about 60 years, until towers were supplanted by airplanes as a means of detecting forest fires.

There is only limited exposure to the elements on Kearsarge North, and the fire tower provides some protection from severe conditions once near the summit. However, hikers should prepare for the possibility of adverse conditions, particularly gusty winds at higher elevations. Spring, summer, and fall are all good seasons for a hike on Kearsarge North. The hike is particularly popular during fall foliage, which generally peaks in late September or early October.

Numerous resorts, hotels, motels, and bed-and-breakfasts are available in North Conway and nearby Jackson. White Mountain National Forest offers a multitude of first-come, first-serve primitive campsites in the surrounding area. North Conway is a popular shopping destination, and several businesses specialize in hiking, climbing, mountaineering, and camping supplies and gear.

17   *Mount Madison*
VALLEY WAY AND OSGOOD TRAILS

GPS Trailhead Coordinates

UTM Zone (WGS 84)	19T
Easting	0317546
Northing	4915477.3
Latitude	N 44° 22'17.88"
Longitude	W 71° 17'22.17"

A view southeast into Crawford Notch from near the Owls Head summit

A mountain tarn on Mount Greylock

Cairns lead south from the summit of Camel's Hump on the Long Trail.

A view from the summit of hikers at the northern end of Knife Edge

A hiker enjoys the views from the summit of Mount Mansfield.

A hiker ascends the Webster-Jackson Trail.

A hiker and his dogs approach the summit of Mount Garfield.

Hikers assemble on the summit of Mount Monadnock.

A view of Ragged Mountain with Mirror Lake in the foreground

A hiker ascends steep ledges near the summit of Potash Mountain.

A hiker nears the summit of South Moat Mountain.

Views north from the summit area on Equinox Mountain

A hiker enjoys the view looking west near the summit of Bear Mountain.

An alpine meadow on Goose Eye Mountain

Mount Washington

A hiker descends from the summit of Camel's Hump on the Long Trail.

🏃 Key Information

LENGTH 7.4 miles

ROUTE CONFIGURATION Out-and-back

DIFFICULTY Difficult

ELEVATION GAIN 4,029 feet

SCENERY Breathtaking views of the Presidentials and the White Mountains

EXPOSURE Considerable exposure to the elements above tree line

TRAIL TRAFFIC Moderate to heavy

TRAIL SURFACE Hard-packed dirt and rock below tree line; boulder-strewn above

CLIMBING TIME 8.5 hours

DRIVING DISTANCE Approximately 110 miles from the junction of Interstate 95 and NH 16 in Portsmouth, NH

ACCESS No fees or permits required

MAPS USGS Quadrangle for Mount Washington

FACILITIES None

WATER REQUIREMENT 2 quarts per person recommended

DOGS ALLOWED Yes

ELEVATION PROFILE

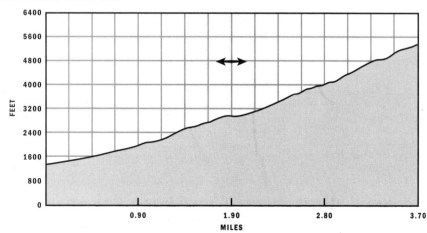

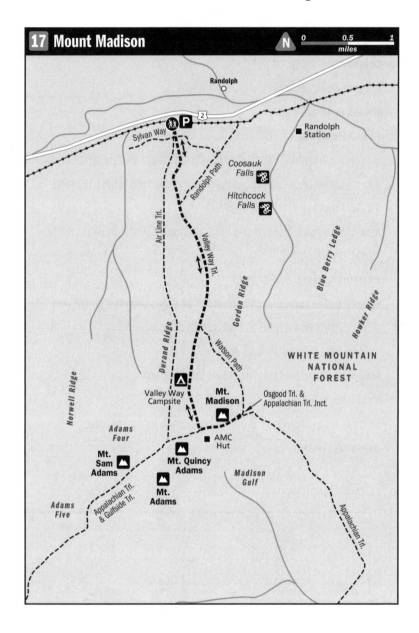

Directions

From the intersection of I-95 and NH 16 in Portsmouth, NH, follow NH 16 (which is also NH 4 and the Spaulding Turnpike, initially) 105.6 miles to US 2 in Gorham. Turn left on US 2 and NH 16 and drive 1.5 miles through the Gorham business district to an intersection where US 2 and NH 16 separate. Turn left on US 2 and continue 5.1 miles to the Appalachia parking area on the left. The trailhead for Valley Way Trail to Mount Madison is on the right side of the parking area next to an information kiosk.

In Brief

Mount Madison, elevation 5,366 feet, is the fifth-highest peak in New England and part of the spectacular Presidential Range. Valley Way Trail is the easiest, shortest, and most sheltered trail to the summit of Mount Madison and the northern Presidentials. Significant boulder scrambling is required on the summit cone, but you will enjoy some of the most magnificent mountain views in the northeastern United States.

Description

From the trailhead, hike easily south on Valley Way and Air Line trails, which subsequently parallel one another to the Gulfside Trail above tree line. Cross a former railroad bed now used as a multiuse rail-trail at 100 yards. At 0.1 mile the Air Line Trail branches off right and ascends to Mount Adams.

Follow Valley Way Trail left on a good hard-packed dirt path in a hardwood and mixed conifer forest to a junction with Sylvan Way Trail at 0.2 miles. Pay particular heed to trail signs and markings in this area because numerous trails diverge and intersect. At 0.5 miles, a side trail loops left past picturesque waterfalls and rejoins Valley Way. At 0.7 miles, pass Beechwood Way junction on the right, then Brookside on the left, and climb to an intersection with Randolph Pass at 0.8 miles.

Continue steadily upward on a trail that is markedly rockier. At 1.2 miles, the gradient increases and persists to the Scar Trail junction on the right at 1.6 miles. At 1.8 miles, dip down slightly to an intersection with Watson Path, a rugged alternate trail to the Mount Madison summit. (I do not recommend taking Watson Path.) Push forward past the Lower Bruin Trail junction on the left at 2.1 miles and arrive at the Valley Way Campsite on the right at 2.7 miles.

Valley Way Campsite, elevation approximately 3,900 feet, is operated by the U.S. Forest Service. The site has two tent platforms and a primitive toilet, but drinking water is not readily available. However, a spring is located 0.1 mile farther up Valley Way Trail; the water must be purified before consumption. Backpacking to the campsite provides an alternative to an out-and-back day hike.

From the campsite, ascend an unrelenting, rocky, narrow trail in a predominantly spruce forest for 0.4 miles. As vegetation becomes more stunted, watch for glimpses of the north slope of Mount Madison to the southeast at 3.1 miles. Hike on through thick mountain scrub and

View of Mount Madison from Mount Adams—Madison Spring Hut in the col

emerge into a clearing at a major trail junction in front of the Madison Spring Hut at 3.4 miles. The hut, elevation approximately 4,800 feet, is operated by the Appalachian Mountain Club (AMC) and is the eastern terminus of the Gulfside Trail. Several other trails converge at or near this junction, including the Osgood Trail leading to the summit of Mount Madison.

The remainder of the climb to the summit is above tree line with significant potential for severe weather. If you encounter adverse conditions, turn back and seek shelter in the hut or below tree line. Many fatalities have occurred due to exposure to the harsh elements in the alpine region of the Presidentials.

Turn left onto Osgood Trail and scale a massive boulder pile. Carefully follow cairns and white blazes, as the route is not obvious. Scramble over and around huge rocks, cross a narrow crest, and drop slightly down the south side of the summit cone. Cautiously continue to edge along a steep, rocky slope while angling upward to an attenuated arête. Follow the rugged ridge easterly to the high point marked with a large cairn at 3.7 miles.

On the summit, savor what are arguably the most magnificent mountain views in the northeastern United States. The majestic, alpine Presidential Range towers dramatically for miles to the southeast—first Mount Adams, then Mount Jefferson, and then the tallest of all, imposing Mount Washington. During summer months, you can usually observe traffic weaving precariously along the precipitous slopes of Mount Washington on the auto road. If weather permits, enjoy a picnic lunch or an extended respite in this mountain paradise.

Cautiously descend the summit cone while enjoying continuous views of Mounts Jefferson, Adams, and the adjunct peak of John Quincy Adams, with the Madison Spring Hut nestled in the col below. If the hut is open, replenish food and water supplies, drop below tree line on Valley Way Trail, and return to Appalachia.

The northern Presidentials provide some of the best and most scenic mountaineering in New England. A multitude of trails ascend the northern slopes of the Presidentials from US 2 at or near the Appalachia trailhead. Additional paths approach from nearby NH 16 in the east.

History, Weather, and Lodging

Mount Madison is named for the fourth president of the United States. It is part of the Presidential Range, which includes the five highest peaks in New England and the northeast: Washington, Adams, Jefferson, Monroe, and Madison. The range is famous for its towering summits, deep ravines, precipitous headwalls, alpine environment, and notoriously mercurial weather.

Madison Spring Hut was the first AMC hut built in the White Mountains. Originally constructed in 1888, it subsequently burned and was rebuilt on the same site in 1941. It sleeps 52 in coed bunkrooms and includes toilets, a source of water, and a small store where snacks and some supplies can be purchased. The AMC maintains several huts along the Appalachian Trail in the White Mountains spaced about a day apart. Madison Spring Hut is generally open during the summer months, and an overnight stay provides a good alternative to an out-and-back day hike. Reservations are required, and more information is available at the AMC Web site at www.outdoors.org.

Mount Madison does not have the same continuous exposure to the elements that Mount Washington and the other Presidential peaks do. However, once above tree line, the same severe weather conditions can occur during any season. Before planning a climb to the summit, secure a reliable summit weather forecast. The best choice for a forecast is the Mount Washington Observatory Web site at www.mountwashington.org. On the day of the hike, obtain a current summit forecast at the AMC Pinkham Notch Visitor Center on NH 16 about 10 miles south of Gorham. Always carry adequate protective gear and clothing to address the potentially extreme climatic variables that can occur in this alpine environment. The best times to climb Mount Madison are during summer and very early fall.

Several motels and bed-and-breakfasts are available in nearby Gorham. You can also obtain lodging at the Pinkham Notch Visitor Center. Besides Valley Way Campsite, camping is available at Moose Brook State Park in Gorham, which has more than 40 well-spaced sites with showers and toilets. Gorham also has retail businesses that specialize in camping, hiking, and mountaineering supplies and gear.

18   *Mount Jackson*
JACKSON-WEBSTER TRAIL

GPS Trailhead Coordinates

UTM Zone (WGS 84)	19T
Easting	0307605.3
Northing	4898362.7
Latitude	N 44° 12'54.42"
Longitude	W 71° 24'28.26"

ᨠ᨞ **Key Information**

LENGTH 4.4 miles

ROUTE CONFIGURATION Out-and-back

DIFFICULTY Easy to moderate

ELEVATION GAIN 2,114 feet

SCENERY Excellent views of Crawford Notch from overlooks and the surrounding White Mountains from the summit

EXPOSURE Limited exposure to the elements in the summit area

TRAIL TRAFFIC Heavy

TRAIL SURFACE Hard-packed dirt and rock; ledge scrambling near summit

CLIMBING TIME 4.5 hours

DRIVING DISTANCE Approximately 110 miles from the junction of Interstate 95 and NH 16 in Portsmouth, NH

ACCESS No fees or permits required

MAPS USGS Quadrangle for Crawford Notch

FACILITIES None

WATER REQUIREMENT 1.5 quarts per person recommended

DOGS ALLOWED Yes

ELEVATION PROFILE

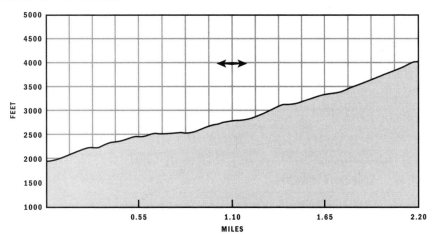

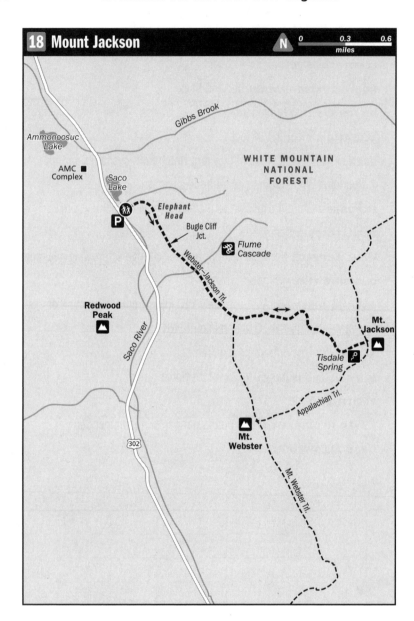

Directions

From the intersection of I-95 and NH 16 in Portsmouth, NH, follow NH 16 (which is also NH 4 and the Spaulding Turnpike, initially) 83 miles to Glen, where US 302 diverges to the left.

A hiker descends from the steep summit of Mount Jackson.

Drive 18.7 miles on US 302 to a parking area on the left in Crawford Notch, 0.3 miles before the Highland Center at Crawford Notch. The trailhead for Webster-Jackson Trail is marked with a sign and located directly across the road from the parking area.

In Brief

Located east of historic Crawford Notch, Mount Jackson, elevation 4,016 feet, is one of the easiest hikes to the summit of a 4,000-footer in the White Mountains. The summit area provides outstanding views of the southern Presidentials, the Willey Range, and beyond. Some rock and ledge scrambling is required near the top.

Description

From the parking area, cross US 302 to the trailhead for Webster-Jackson Trail. Enter a mixed hardwood and conifer forest and hike easily on a hard-packed dirt and rock path. At 0.1 mile, a

A hiker crosses Cascade Flume on the Webster-Jackson Trail.

spur trail goes right to Elephant Head Overlook. This easy 0.2-mile walk to the broad, almost flat ledge overlooking Crawford Notch is worth the effort, with its outstanding views of the notch.

Ascend on a gentle upward gradient for 0.3 miles, then turn to the right on a flat section of trail. At 0.5 miles, angle left and climb the steep, boulder-strewn trail toward a large rock formation. Pass under and to the right of the huge stone overhang and arrive at a side trail on the right. This trail leads to Bugle Cliff Overlook at 0.6 miles. Scramble 40 yards over a sloping ledge for exceptional views of Crawford Notch from the edge of the precipice.

Hike easily for 0.2 miles to a stream crossing, Flume Cascade, which tumbles dramatically down to the west. Cautiously traverse the substantial, slanted rocks on the cascade to re-enter the forested area. Climb more steadily for 0.5 miles to a junction where the Webster-Jackson Trail diverges at 1.3 miles.

Turn left on the Jackson branch and ascend precipitously on a damp, root-exposed, and boulder-strewn path in a predominantly spruce-fir forest. Cross Silver Cascade at 1.6 miles and enter stunted spruce growth, which offers sporadic views of the barren summit of Mount

Jackson at 2.1 miles. Angle left and scramble over a near-vertical ledge to emerge above tree line. Follow cairns and blue blazes and scale a huge, oblique boulder for 75 yards to the summit cairn at 2.2 miles.

At the summit, enjoy expansive vistas of the southern Presidentials to the northeast. A rocky ridge extends southwest from the summit to Mount Webster. The Willey range looms on the west side of the notch, with Franconia Ridge beyond. Glimpses of Crawford Notch are visible looking down to the northwest. Carefully descend the steep summit ledges and return to the trailhead in Crawford Notch.

A loop trip over the summit of Mount Webster is possible. From the top of Mount Jackson, hike southwest on Webster Cliff Trail along the rugged ridge connecting Jackson with Mount Webster. At 1.1 miles, arrive at the Webster branch trail junction on the right. To reach the apex of Mount Webster and the dramatic Webster Cliffs, continue for 0.1 mile on Webster Cliff Trail. Return and descend steadily on the Webster branch, passing below spectacular Silver Cascade just before reaching the Webster-Jackson Trail junction after 0.8 miles. Drop northwesterly on Webster-Jackson Trail for 1.3 miles to Crawford Notch. Do not attempt this loop trip during bad weather because of the considerable exposure to the elements on the ridge between Mounts Jackson and Webster.

Great hiking options abound in the Crawford Notch area. Just north of the Webster-Jackson trailhead on US 302, Avalon Trail leads west to the Willey Range and the White Mountains beyond. Opposite Avalon Trail, Crawford Path departs to the Presidentials in the east. Several additional trails leave US 302 south of the notch.

History, Weather, and Lodging

The history of Crawford Notch is a rich part of White Mountain lore. The Crawford family settled near the head of the notch late in the 18th century. Despite great difficulties and hardships, they survived and flourished in this harsh, mountainous environment. One of the more famous family members, Abel Crawford, constructed and operated an inn called Mount Crawford House and pioneered the famous Crawford Path to the summit of Mount Washington in the early 19th century.

Ironically, although part of the Presidential Range, Mount Jackson is not named for President Andrew Jackson, but instead for a prominent 19th-century New Hampshire geologist, Charles Thomas Jackson. Mount Webster is named for famous American statesman Daniel Webster.

Exposure to the elements on Mount Jackson is limited to less than 0.1 mile above tree line. However, gusting winds on the summit, particularly from the northwest, can be fierce, and climbers should carry adequate protective clothing for that eventuality. The best time for a hike on Mount Jackson is spring through fall.

Numerous resorts, hotels, motels, and bed-and-breakfasts are in nearby Twin Mountain and farther south on US 302 in North Conway. You can also obtain lodging at the Highland Center in Crawford Notch, and camping is available in Twin Mountain and south along US 302.

19

Mount Monadnock
WHITE DOT, WHITE CROSS, AND SPRUCE LINK TRAILS LOOP

GPS Trailhead Coordinates

UTM Zone (WGS 84)	18T
Easting	0737835.4
Northing	4747578.1
Latitude	N 42° 50'44.88"
Longitude	W 72° 05'20.59"

🚶 Key Information

LENGTH 3.6 miles

ROUTE CONFIGURATION Out-and-back with an inner loop

DIFFICULTY Moderate

ELEVATION GAIN A little less than 1,800 feet

SCENERY Exceptional views of southern New Hampshire and northern Massachusetts

EXPOSURE Considerable exposure to the elements

TRAIL TRAFFIC Heavy

TRAIL SURFACE Hard-packed dirt and rock at lower elevations; extensive ledge scrambling at higher elevations

CLIMBING TIME 4 hours

DRIVING DISTANCE Approximately 37 miles from the junction of US 3 and NH 101A in Nashua, NH

ACCESS Day-use or camping fee required

MAPS USGS Quadrangle for Monadnock Mountain

FACILITIES Restrooms with toilets and showers at the trailhead

WATER REQUIREMENT 1.5 quarts per person recommended

DOGS ALLOWED No

ELEVATION PROFILE

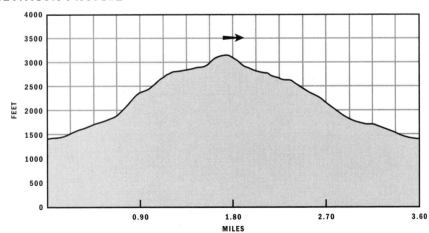

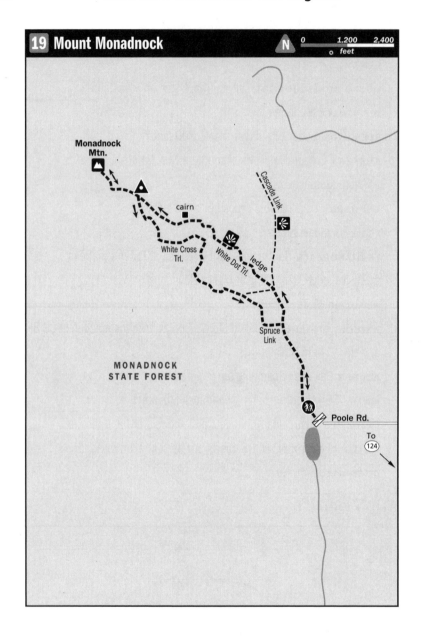

Directions

From the intersection of US 3 and NH 101A in Nashua, NH, follow NH 101A west 8.2 miles to NH 101 in Milford. Turn left onto NH 101 and drive 18 miles to US 202 in Peterborough. Turn left onto US 202 and go south 5.5 miles to NH 124 in Jaffrey. Turn right onto NH 124 and drive 2.2 miles. Turn right onto Dublin Road (also Monadnock Mountain Road) and go 1.2 miles. Turn left on Poole Road and drive 0.8 miles to the Monadnock State Park tollgate. Parking is on the left just after the tollgate, and the trailhead is 150 yards straight up the road past the campground entrance, restrooms, and visitor center, all on the right.

In Brief

Located in south-central New Hampshire, Mount Monadnock, elevation 3,137 feet, is the most popular hike in New England. Epitomizing the definition of a monadnock, a mountain that stands isolated or alone, much of the climb is over open ledges with spectacular views of southern New Hampshire and northern Massachusetts. Expect extended ledge scrambling at higher elevations.

Description

From the White Dot trailhead, hike easily on a wide, well-maintained, rock and hard-packed dirt path in a deciduous forest for 0.4 miles to the Spruce Link Trail junction. The inner-loop trip begins and ends here. Ascending White Dot Trail is recommended because White Cross and Spruce Link trails provide a more gradual and normally safer descent.

Scramble over a couple of gentle ledges, continue hiking easily, and arrive at a trail junction for White Cross and Cascade trails at 0.6 miles. Climb steeply on rocky terrain and reach an extended, up-sloping rock formation at 0.7 miles. Carefully negotiate this precipitous, multi-level projection in the shade of large, overhanging maple trees. Continue steadily up a boulder-strewn surface, clamber over and around a rugged rock face, and reach a viewpoint looking south at 0.9 miles. From this location, enjoy expansive vistas of the ponds, pastures, and hills of northern Massachusetts.

Continue less arduously through patchy spruce growth and emerge above tree line at a large cairn, elevation 2,797 feet, at 1.2 miles. Pause to appreciate the outstanding views to the south and east. Recommence hiking over granite ledges in spotty, stunted conifer growth and arrive at the Red Spot Connector Trail junction, painted in red on a large boulder, at 1.4 miles. From this vantage point, glimpse the barren, rounded summit farther north.

Hike easily on ledges in sporadic spruce growth to the White Cross Trail junction, marked with a wooden sign, at 1.5 miles. This is the northern terminus of the inner-loop trip. Snake circuitously upward on exposed rock and ledge following cairns and white blazes toward the summit. Angle slightly northeast through a narrow slot in the rocks, turn left, and scramble up a sloping rock face to the top at 1.7 miles.

Hikers nearing the summit of Mount Monadnock

From the summit of the monadnock, savor phenomenal 360-degree views. A long, partially barren ridge runs north toward Dublin Lake. The lakes, ponds, pastures, and small hills below seem to peer up in homage from all directions. On a clear day, the tall buildings of Boston are visible on the eastern horizon, and the outline of Mount Greylock, the highest point in Massachusetts, can be observed in the southwest.

Backtrack on White Dot Trail and carefully descend huge boulders and ledges for 0.2 miles to the White Cross Trail junction on the right. Turn right and drop into a protected forested area, which can also provide limited shelter from the elements in an emergency. Hike 0.4 miles to Bald Rock Overlook, which offers exceptional views to the southwest, at 2.3 miles. Continue down a rocky, stairwaylike path for 0.5 miles while glimpsing sporadic views to the south and east. Reach a junction with Spruce Link Trail on the right at 2.8 miles.

Turn right on Spruce Link Trail and drop gradually on a predominantly hard-packed dirt surface to the White Dot Trail junction at 3.2 miles. Hike easily on White Dot Trail for the remaining 0.4 miles to the original trailhead. Stop at the visitor center on the left and view the interesting exhibits regarding the park's history and ecology.

With over 40 miles of maintained trails, Mount Monadnock State Park is a mountaineer's paradise with a multitude of climbing opportunities. Monadnock Sunapee Trail leaves from Old Troy Road in Dublin and ascends to the summit from the northwest. Approaching over the ridge from Dublin Lake in the north is the Pumpelly Trail. Marlboro Trail begins on Shaker Road in the west and connects with Monadnock Sunapee Trail near the summit, and the Old Halfway House Trail begins at the park gate 3 miles west of the entrance to Dublin Road on NH 124 and joins a labyrinth of interconnecting paths south of the summit. From the east, Birchtoft Trail begins at a parking area on Dublin Road and climbs to Red Spot and Pumpelly trails to reach the top.

History, Weather, and Lodging

Is Mount Monadnock the world's most frequently climbed mountain or is that a distinction that rightfully belongs to Mount Fuji in Japan? Sources differ, but regardless, Mount Monadnock is one of the most popular hikes in the entire world. First climbed by European settlers early in the 18th century, it has been a favored hiking destination for nearly 200 years. Famous author, poet, and philosopher Henry David Thoreau often visited Mount Monadnock in the mid-19th century. Today, thousands follow in his footsteps each year.

Monadnock State Park Campground provides an excellent base camp for hiking the numerous mountain trails in the park. It has 28 campsites; some may be reserved, while others are first-come, first-serve, and the remaining sites are for youth groups. Flush toilets, showers, and a camp store are available. The campground is generally open from late May through early October. For additional information on camping in the state park, call (603) 532-8862 or access the New Hampshire State Parks Web site at www.nhparks.nh.us.

Potentially adverse weather conditions are a risk on Mount Monadnock during any season. Hikers will encounter considerable exposure to the elements above tree line. Obtain a reliable mountain weather forecast prior to a planned climb and always carry sufficient protective clothing and gear to address potential weather hazards. Check the mountain forecast with rangers at the tollgate on the day of the hike. Spring, summer, and fall are all good seasons for a climb on Mount Monadnock.

Lodging is limited in the immediate Mount Monadnock area. However, hotels, motels, and bed-and-breakfasts are plentiful in the nearby communities of Peterborough and Keene. Numerous campgrounds are available in the greater Peterborough area. Perhaps the best camping option is the Monadnock State Park Campground.

20   *Mount Washington*

TUCKERMAN RAVINE TRAIL

GPS Trailhead Coordinates

UTM Zone (WGS 84)	19T
Easting	0320710
Northing	4903780
Latitude	N 44° 15'26.22"
Longitude	W 71° 15'9.72"

👣 Key Information

LENGTH 7.2 miles

ROUTE CONFIGURATION Out-and-back

DIFFICULTY Difficult

ELEVATION GAIN Exceeds 4,200 feet

SCENERY Spectacular above-tree line views of the White Mountains and northern New England

EXPOSURE Considerable above-tree line exposure to the elements

TRAIL TRAFFIC Busy

TRAIL SURFACE Dirt below Hermit Lake Shelters; rocky and boulder-strewn above

CLIMBING TIME 8 hours

DRIVING DISTANCE Approximately 100 miles from the junction of Interstate 95 and NH 16 in Portsmouth, NH

ACCESS No fees or permits required

MAPS USGS Mount Washington Quadrangle; trail maps available at the Pinkham Notch Visitor Center at the trailhead

FACILITIES Restrooms, lodging, restaurant, showers, supplies, phone, and weather information available at the Pinkham Notch Visitor Center at the trailhead

WATER REQUIREMENT Two quarts per person recommended

DOGS ALLOWED Yes

ELEVATION PROFILE

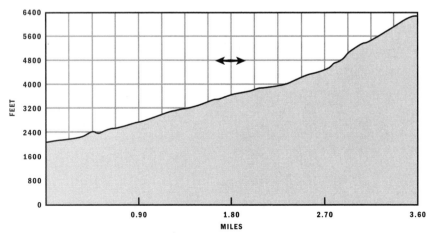

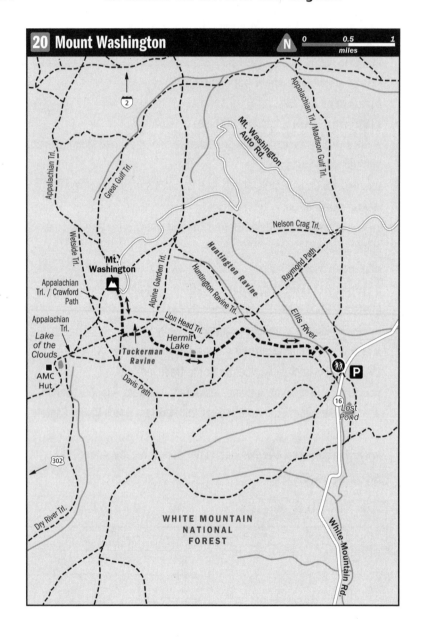

20 Mount Washington

N   0   0.5   1
          miles

Mt. Washington Auto Rd.

Appalachian Trl./Madison Gulf Trl.

Appalachian Trl.

Great Gulf Trl.

Nelson Crag Trl.

Westside Trl.

Mt. Washington

Alpine Garden Trl.

Huntington Ravine

Huntington Ravine Trl.

Raymond Path

Appalachian Trl. / Crawford Path

Ellis River

Appalachian Trl.

Lion Head Trl.

Lake of the Clouds

Hermit Lake

AMC Hut

Tuckerman Ravine

Davis Path

P

302

16   *Lost Pond*

Dry River Trl.

WHITE MOUNTAIN NATIONAL FOREST

White Mountain Rd.

Directions

From the intersection of I-95 and NH 16 in Portsmouth, NH, follow NH 16 (which is also NH 4 and the Spaulding Turnpike, initially) 85 miles to Jackson. Drive 9.4 miles farther north on NH 16 to the Pinkham Notch Visitor Center on the left. A large parking area sits in front of the main building. The trailhead for Tuckerman Ravine Trail is located directly behind the main building.

In Brief

Mount Washington is the highest peak in the northeastern United States. Some rock and boulder scrambling is required at higher elevations. Expect significant exposure to cold, wind, sun, and rain above tree line, and remember that severe weather can be a risk. The summit area provides spectacular 360-degree views of northern New England.

Description

From the trailhead, hike easily up a tractor road that ascends gradually through a dense evergreen forest for 2.1 miles to Hermit Lake Shelters. Pass several side trails along the way, including Huntington Ravine Trail at 1.2 miles and Lion Head at 1.9 miles. Both trails provide alternative, but more difficult, routes to the summit. As you gain elevation, glimpses of the towering cliffs of Tuckerman Ravine become more frequent. Finally, the cliff's full majesty abruptly appears at a clearing in front of HoJo's, the caretaker's cabin at Hermit Lake Shelters.

Lean-to and tent camping are permitted at Hermit Lake, and you can purchase reservation tickets at the visitor center. Hermit Lake is a popular destination for backpackers and offers accommodations for up to 86 people. Primitive toilets and running water are available during spring and summer.

Depart Hermit Lake and continue north for about a half mile to the cirque at the foot of the ravine where the headwall dominates the landscape. Here, begin to weave your way steeply up the rock-faced precipice. Near the base of the headwall at a shaded area called Snow Arch, snow often lingers well into the summer months. Exercise extra caution if large accumulations of snow or ice are present, as there may be a danger of avalanche. Although this portion of the trail ascends quite precipitously, it is well designed and has a stairwaylike character. However, footing can be treacherous when wet or during stormy weather.

Shortly after emerging from the ravine, pass Alpine Garden Trail on the right and arrive at Tuckerman Junction at mile 3.1. Several converging trails intersect at this juncture, so pay careful attention to trail signs to remain on the correct trail. Above the ravine is an alpine zone, where weather conditions can change rapidly at any time of year. If stormy weather threatens, descend immediately below tree line. To reach the summit from Tuckerman Junction, follow the cairns as the trail climbs steadily up a steep boulder field for a half mile. With buildings and towers chained to the ground in an environment that could otherwise pass as moonscape, the summit often shocks the sensibilities of hiking purists with its circuslike atmosphere.

A hiker ascends Tuckerman Ravine.

Up top, there is a weather observatory and a visitor center with a restaurant and observation deck, but lodging is not available. Tourists arriving via an auto road or the historic Mount Washington Cog Railway add to the carnival effect. They wander about the structures and walkways in the summit area, often staring in disbelief at arriving hikers. Despite the distractions, hikers should take time to scramble up the rock pile that constitutes the true summit and feast upon the views of New England from the top. Tour the famous Tip Top House (if open)—it's made of stone blasted from mountain rock, which is only a few feet away. Allow ample time to ensure a safe descent to Pinkham Notch during daylight hours.

After summiting, many hikers continue in a southwesterly direction and descend the Crawford Path for about 1.5 miles to the Appalachian Mountain Club (AMC) Lakes-in-the-Clouds Hut. The hut, where overnight lodging is possible, is located just above tree line within view of the summit and at the foot of barren Mount Monroe. Two small alpine tarns are nearby. Advance reservations are required to stay at the AMC hut. For information, access their Web site at www.outdoors.org.

To reconnect with Tuckerman Junction without backtracking over the summit, return 200 yards on the Crawford Path and then turn right onto Crossover Trail. Follow it northeasterly for 0.7 miles to Tuckerman Junction. Another option is to descend Ammonoosuc Ravine Trail from the hut to a parking area near the Cog Railway departure station. The AMC operates a shuttle service that connects the Ammonoosuc Ravine Trailhead with the Pinkham Notch Visitor Center. For more shuttle information, including a schedule, again visit www.outdoors.org.

History, Weather, and Lodging

Mount Washington's rich history includes the first-known successful climb, which was accomplished by explorer Darby Field in 1642. The Crawford family, who settled in nearby Crawford Notch at the end of the 18th century, pioneered a trail from the notch to the summit, the present-day Crawford Path. Later they converted it to a bridle path, leading to a hotel near the summit. In 1869 engineers constructed the Mount Washington Cog Railway, reputed to be the world's first mountain-climbing cog railway. The railway still operates several months a year. All the early summit structures burned in a fire in 1908 except the Tip Top House, which probably survived because of its rock exterior. The auto road to the summit, completed in 1861, was originally built for horse- and ox-drawn wagons. In 1899 Freelan Stanley drove the first vehicle to the top: a Stanley Steamer. The auto road is now open for traffic during the summer months and is the site of annual bicycle, foot, and auto races. Today, the 2,175-mile Appalachian Trail passes over Mount Washington primarily following the Crawford Path.

During the week and day prior to climbing Mount Washington, climbers should obtain a reliable mountain weather forecast. Literature boasts that it has the world's worst weather. While this may be a bit of an exaggeration, its weather, especially in winter, has been likened to that of Antarctica. Some Mount Washington Weather Observatory data is absolutely astounding. The highest wind speed ever recorded on the surface of the earth, 231 miles per hour, occurred on the summit in 1934. Mount Washington receives hurricane-force winds an average of 104 days per year. An excellent source of information on summit weather conditions is the Mount Washington Observatory Web site at www.mountwashington.org, and climbers should make a final weather check at the Pinkham Notch Visitor Center prior to departure.

All hikers should have solid orienteering skills, including the ability to effectively use a map and compass, and should consider carrying a GPS. Even during summer, fast-moving storms can rapidly create wintry conditions that are extremely disorienting and potentially dangerous. Thick cloud cover can quickly envelop the whole mountain in minutes, reducing visibility to a few feet.

The Mount Washington area is a mountaineering paradise. Scores of well-maintained mountain trails are scattered throughout the White Mountains and provide convenient avenues for travel to the summit of almost every peak. Numerous resorts, hotels, motels, and bed-and-breakfasts are in the surrounding towns of Gorham, North Conway, Jackson, and Twin Mountain. Besides Pinkham Notch and Lakes-in-the-Clouds, the AMC provides overnight lodging in its hut system throughout the White Mountains and at the Crawford Notch Visitor Center. Camping is available at Moose Brook State Park in Gorham. North Conway is a well-known shopping destination with dozens of outlet stores and several outfitting retailers that cater to hikers and climbers.

21 *Cherry Mountain:* Owls Head (North Peak)
OWLS HEAD TRAIL

GPS Trailhead Coordinates

UTM Zone (WGS 84)	19T
Easting	0301696.3
Northing	4914668.5
Latitude	N 44° 21'36.72"
Longitude	W 71° 29'16.58"

🏃 Key Information

LENGTH 4.8 miles

ROUTE CONFIGURATION Out-and-back

DIFFICULTY Easy to moderate

ELEVATION GAIN Just over 2,000 feet

SCENERY Outstanding views of the Presidentials and Crawford Notch from the summit

EXPOSURE Very little exposure to the elements

TRAIL TRAFFIC Light

TRAIL SURFACE Dirt and rock

CLIMBING TIME 4.5 hours

DRIVING DISTANCE Approximately 95 miles from the junction of Interstates 93 and 89 in Concord, NH

ACCESS No fees or permits required

MAPS USGS Quadrangle for Mount Washington

FACILITIES None

WATER REQUIREMENT 1.5 quarts per person recommended

DOGS ALLOWED Yes

ELEVATION PROFILE

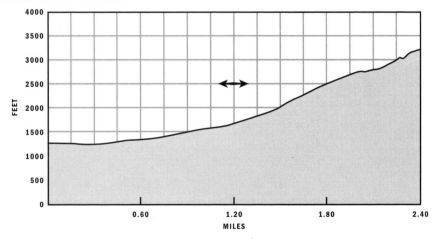

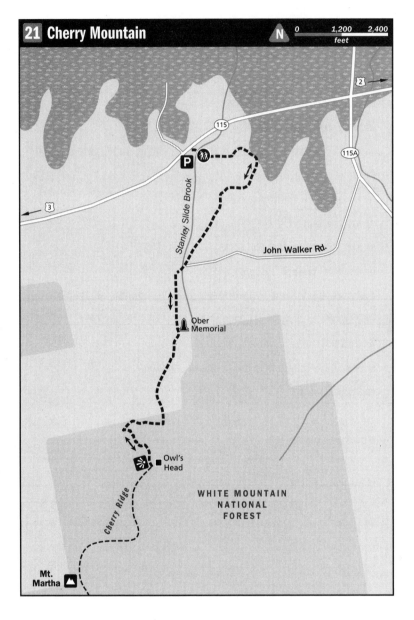

A hiker on the Owls Head Trail

Directions

From the intersection of I-93 and I-89 in Concord, NH, follow I-93 north 76.9 miles to the exit for NH 3 in Franconia. Go straight on NH 3 10.4 miles to an intersection with US 302 in Twin Mountain. Cross US 302 and continue 2 miles on NH 3. In Carroll, turn right on NH 115 and drive 6.2 miles to a parking area on the right. The trailhead for Owls Head Trail is on the left side of the parking area and marked with a sign.

In Brief

Cherry Mountain lies a few miles west of the Presidential Range in north-central New Hampshire. The summit of Owls Head (the north peak of Cherry Mountain), elevation 3,263 feet, provides excellent views of the Presidentials, Crawford Notch, and the peaks surrounding Franconia Notch.

A hiker nears the summit of Owls Head.

Description

From the trailhead, walk under a canopy of ancient crab apple trees on the Owls Head Trail, cross a small brook, and go 50 yards on an old farm road to a sign on the left that reads "Path." Turn left, follow yellow blazes, and hike easily in a low-lying, damp, swampy area with an abundant population of partridge for 0.5 miles.

At 0.6 miles, ascend more steadily on a dry, hard-packed dirt trail surrounded by prodigious ferns in a new-growth hardwood forest. Cross Stanley Slide Brook at 0.9 miles, clamber up a steep bank, and intersect with gravel John Walker Road at 1 mile. Reenter the hardwood forest and continue gradually upwards to a memorial sign for Kit Ober, a young woman who died in 1979, located in an impressive stand of tall maples at 1.3 miles.

The path of loose stones, dirt, and some exposed tree roots climbs steeply and unrelentingly for 0.6 miles. At 1.9 miles, angle sharply right in a boulder-strewn section and continue laterally beneath and north of the Owls Head summit for 0.3 miles. At 2.2 miles advance higher via short, abrupt switchbacks and scramble up a precipitous, sloping ledge to the Owls Head summit, which is marked with a wooden sign attached to a tree at 2.4 miles.

For spectacular views to the south, east, and west, continue down through patchy, stunted spruce growth for 30 yards to several levels of almost flat, tablelike ledges spaced a few feet apart. From this vantage point, Cherry Mountain's south peak, spruce-covered Mount Martha, looms directly ahead. The Presidential Range, the highest mountain ridge in the northeastern United States, towers majestically in the east, ending dramatically in nearby Crawford Notch. The equally spectacular peaks of Garfield and Franconia ridges dominate the horizon in the southwest. Select the granite shelf that provides the best combination of shelter and visibility for a long, leisurely picnic lunch before returning to Owls Head Trailhead.

Hiking south to the summit of Mount Martha and beyond is possible. However, the trail is rugged and the Mount Martha summit lacks comparable views, so I don't recommend this alternative. Several additional hikes are available on the Cherry Mountain Range. Cherry Mountain Trail begins 4 miles farther south of Owls Head Trailhead on NH 115, traverses Mount Martha, and descends to Old Cherry Mountain Road in the east. Black Brook Trail leaves from US 302 in the south and joins Cherry Mountain Trail a little south of the summit of Mount Martha.

History, Weather, and Lodging

The Owls Head Trail area was the site of a catastrophic landslide in 1885. According to an information sign located near the trailhead, the slide crashed down the mountain for more than 2 miles and destroyed Oscar Stanley's farm located nearby. His house, barn, cattle, and crops were totally engulfed. A farmhand perished, but, miraculously, the family survived.

Normally, exposure to adverse climatic conditions is not a problem when climbing Owls Head on Cherry Mountain because Owls Head Trail is completely below tree line. The hike is not recommended in spring or during periods of high water because the swampy area can become immersed in mud and water and Stanley Slide Brook may be impassable. The best times for a hike to the summit of Owls Head are summer and fall.

Camping is available in the nearby towns of Twin Mountain, Gorham, and Franconia. An excellent camping choice is Moose Brook State Park in Gorham, with more than 40 well-spaced tent sites and hot showers. A multitude of resorts, hotels, motels, and bed-and-breakfasts are located in Twin Mountain and Gorham.

22   *Mount Garfield*
GARFIELD TRAIL

GPS Trailhead Coordinates

UTM Zone (WGS 84)	19T
Easting	0289616.2
Northing	4900250.9
Latitude	N 44° 13'37.68"
Longitude	W 71° 38'0.84"

🥾 Key Information

LENGTH 8.3 miles

ROUTE CONFIGURATION Out-and-back

DIFFICULTY Moderate

ELEVATION GAIN Just over 3,000 feet

SCENERY From the summit, extensive 360-degree views of the White Mountains

EXPOSURE Some exposure to the elements at the summit

TRAIL TRAFFIC Light to moderate

TRAIL SURFACE Hard-packed dirt below Garfield Ridge Trail; boulder-strewn above the ridge

CLIMBING TIME 7 hours

DRIVING DISTANCE Approximately 83 miles from the junction of Interstates 93 and 89 in Concord, NH

ACCESS Day-use parking fee required

MAPS USGS Quadrangles for Franconia and South Twin Mountain

FACILITIES None

WATER REQUIREMENT 1.5 quarts per person recommended

DOGS ALLOWED Yes

ELEVATION PROFILE

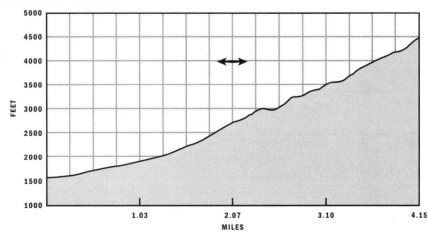

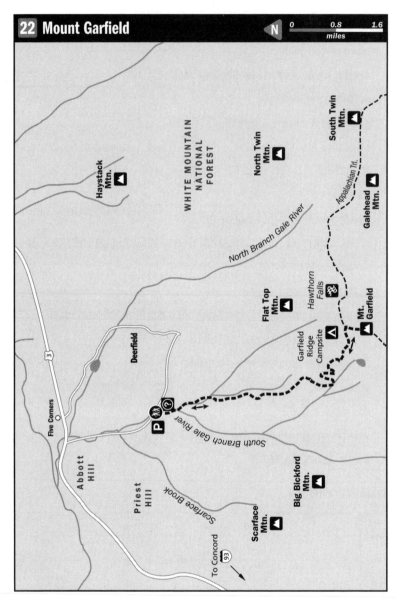

22 Mount Garfield

N 0 0.8 1.6
miles

Haystack Mtn.

WHITE MOUNTAIN NATIONAL FOREST

North Twin Mtn.

South Twin Mtn.

Appalachian Trl.

Galehead Mtn.

North Branch Gale River

Flat Top Mtn.

Hawthorn Falls

Mt. Garfield

Garfield Ridge Campsite

Deerfield

Five Corners

3

South Branch Gale River

Abbott Hill

Priest Hill

Scarface Brook

Scarface Mtn.

Big Bickford Mtn.

To Concord

93

A stream crossing on the Garfield Trail

Directions

From the intersection of I-93 and I-89 in Concord, NH, follow I-93 north 76.9 miles to the exit for NH 3 in Franconia. Go straight on NH 3 4.9 miles to Gale River Loop Road on the right. Turn right on this good gravel road and drive 1.2 miles to a parking area on the right. A self-pay fee station is located on the right side of the parking area. The trailhead for Garfield Trail begins next to an information kiosk.

In Brief

Located north of Franconia Notch, the summit of distinctive Mount Garfield, elevation 4,500 feet, was formerly the site of the Mount Garfield Fire Tower. The high point provides outstanding 360-degree views of New Hampshire's White Mountains. Expect some rock scrambling in the last 0.2 miles before reaching the summit.

A hiker scrambles up a section of the Garfield Ridge Trail near the summit of Mount Garfield.

Description

From the trailhead, clamber up a dirt bank and hike easily south on the Garfield Trail through a beautiful stand of tall hemlocks and spruce. In recent years, storms have toppled numerous hemlocks, so you may have to do some stump-jumping. At 0.5 miles, complete the first of three stream crossings over Thompson Brook.

Near Thompson Brook, connect with the remains of the former fire tower access road and continue to hike easily in a mixed hardwood and conifer forest on a hard-packed dirt surface. At 0.8 miles, make two successive stream traverses and persist on a gentle gradient while following blue blazes.

Beginning at 1.4 miles, the trail ascends more steeply in a southeasterly direction for 0.9 miles. Turn sharply to the southwest at 2.3 miles and hike effortlessly below the northwest ridge of Mount Garfield. Starting at 2.7 miles, persist steadily up the ridge via switchbacks in a predominantly coniferous forest for 1.2 miles to Garfield Ridge Trail at 3.9 miles.

Garfield Ridge Trail is part of the 2,170-mile Appalachian Trial that begins in Georgia and ends on Mount Katahdin in Maine. To reach Garfield Ridge Campsite, turn left and descend steeply for 0.2 miles. The site has a 12-person lean-to shelter, seven tent platforms, a primitive toilet, a source for water, and is operated by the Appalachian Mountain Club. It is a backpacking destination and an alternative to the out-and-back day hike.

Turn right on Garfield Ridge Trail and scramble up and through an abrupt boulder-strewn path in patchy, stunted spruce growth for the next 0.2 miles. Emerge above tree line, hike through an opening in the scrub to the left, and climb several broad, oblique rock shelves to the summit of Mount Garfield, elevation 4,500 feet, at 4.15 miles.

The foundation for the old fire tower is at the very top of the rock formation with 360-degree views. The summit is an excellent location for a picnic lunch surrounded by the peaks of the White Mountains. Franconia Ridge is to the south, Cannon Mountain and the Kinsman Range to the west, Cherry Mountain to the north, and the Twins, Galehead, and the Bonds to the east—the ideal spot for a fire tower.

Carefully climb down the summit ledges, turn left, and find a wide, horizontal boulder facing south with a stunning view of Franconia Ridge. Leave the overlook, turn right on Garfield Ridge Trail, and descend precipitously to the Garfield Trail junction. A loop trip is possible by hiking north on Garfield Ridge Trail 2.5 miles and descending 4 miles on Gale River Trail. However, I don't recommend this alternative, as it is very rugged going on the ridge between Garfield and Gale River trails, and a 2-mile walk or shuttle is required on Gale River Loop Road.

Besides Gale River Trail, numerous other hikes are available in the Mount Garfield area. Nearby Franconia Notch offers an abundance of outstanding trails, and farther north on NH 3 in the Twin Mountain area, paths lead to the Twins, Hale, and Zealand mountains.

History, Weather, and Lodging

The Mount Garfield Fire Tower was built in 1940 and operated by the White Mountain National Forest for eight years. It burned in the 1950s, and only the foundation remains. Perhaps its most famous fire-spotter was a young Frederick Milan, who worked in the tower after graduating from high school in the summer of 1942. He went on to become a renowned anthropologist, mountaineer, and skier.

Because most of the hike is below tree line, exposure to adverse weather is not normally a significant problem. At the summit, the fire tower foundation provides some shelter from gusty winds, and the tree line is just a few yards away. The best times to climb Mount Garfield are summer and early fall. Stream crossings can be problematic during periods of high water, particularly during spring runoff.

A multitude of resorts, hotels, motels, and bed-and-breakfasts are available in the nearby towns of Lincoln and Twin Mountain. Campgrounds are located in Franconia Notch and Twin Mountain. Several businesses in Lincoln retail camping, hiking, and mountaineering clothing, gear, and supplies.

23 *South and North Baldface Mountains*
BALDFACE CIRCLE TRAIL

GPS Trailhead Coordinates

UTM Zone (WGS 84)	19T
Easting	0338901.9
Northing	4900079.8
Latitude	N 44° 14'17.34"
Longitude	W 71° 01'0.75"

🥾 Key Information

LENGTH 8.7 miles

ROUTE CONFIGURATION Loop

DIFFICULTY Moderately difficult

ELEVATION GAIN Exceeds 3,300 feet

SCENERY Exceptional and extended views of Evans Notch area, Wild River Valley, Carter Range, and Mount Washington

EXPOSURE Considerable exposure to the elements

TRAIL TRAFFIC Light to moderate

TRAIL SURFACE Hard-packed dirt and rock at lower elevations; steep ledge and boulder at higher elevations

CLIMBING TIME 8 hours

DRIVING DISTANCE Approximately 100 miles from the junction of Interstate 95 and NH 16 in Portsmouth, NH

ACCESS No fees or permits required

MAPS USGS Quadrangles for Chatham and Wild River

FACILITIES Primitive toilets at trailhead

WATER REQUIREMENT 2 quarts per person recommended

DOGS ALLOWED Yes

ELEVATION PROFILE

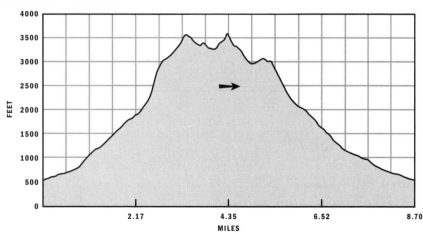

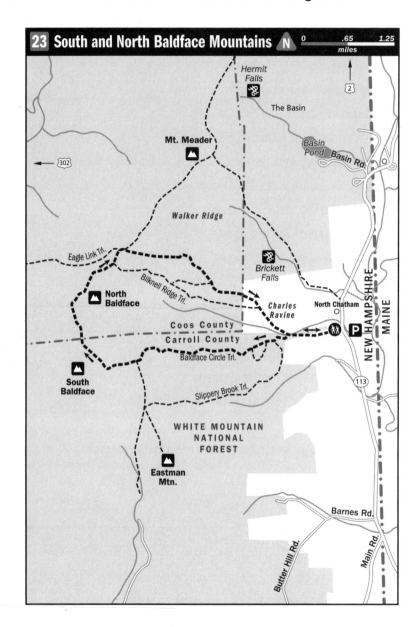

Directions

From the intersection of I-95 and NH 16 in Portsmouth, NH, follow NH 16 (which is also NH 4 and the Spaulding Turnpike, initially) for 75.1 miles to Conway. Leave NH 16 and drive straight on NH 113 for 2 miles to US 302. Go straight on US 302 (crossing the state line into

Maine) for 6.5 miles. Turn left onto NH 113 and drive 16.4 miles north (recrossing the boundary into New Hampshire) to a parking area on the right. The trailhead for Baldface Circle Trail is on the opposite side of the road from the parking area 200 feet north on NH 113.

In Brief

Arguably the best loop trip in New England, the rugged, spectacular Baldface Circle Trip traverses a 4-mile exposed ridge and two barren mountain summits with elevations of 3,570 and 3,610 feet. Views from the ridge are continuous and include Mount Washington, Carter Range, Wild River Valley, and peaks of Evans Notch. Expect substantial steep ledge and boulder scrambling, particularly on the east slope of South Baldface.

Description

From NH 113, scale a steep bank and hike easily in a mixed conifer and hardwood forest on hard-packed dirt Baldface Circle Trail for 0.7 miles to the Circle Trail junction. Clockwise is the recommended loop direction because an ascent of the steep ledges of South Baldface is normally safer than a descent. Turn left and climb more steadily on a wide, well-defined path for 0.3 miles to the Slippery Brook Trail junction on the left at 1 mile. Slippery Brook Trail connects with Baldface Knob Trail, an alternative route to the summit of South Baldface, to avoid the steep ledges on the eastern slope. However, I don't recommend this route because it adds an extra mile of hiking to the loop and deprives climbers of the spectacular views from the ledges. It is a good option when conditions are wet or icy.

At 1.1 miles, Chandler Gorge Loop Trail departs to the left. This 0.5-mile spur circles past a narrow gorge with a waterfall and several smaller cataracts. It returns to Baldface Circle Trail at 1.3 miles.

Continue steeply on Baldface Circle Trail. This section of trail is part of an old logging road for 0.9 miles. At 2.2 miles, turn slightly to the right and scramble over and around a boulder-strewn section of path on the southwest slope of a height of land. At 2.4 miles arrive at South Baldface Shelter, where there is a lean-to, space for tents, and a primitive toilet. For many, the shelter is a backpacking destination.

Hike beyond the shelter and emerge at the base of the South Baldface ledges. Climbing the ledges when wet or icy is hazardous and not recommended. When dangerous conditions exist, backtrack to Slippery Brook Trail to take the alternative route to the South Baldface summit.

Climb cautiously in a westerly direction on steep ledges in patchy mountain scrub. Carefully follow blue blazes and cairns while weaving slowly up a series of large, slanting rock formations and projections for 0.2 miles. Glance back to the east to appreciate the outstanding views of the peaks of Evans Notch. Angle to the left and edge southwesterly around a significant granite overhang and clamber up loose rocks and boulders to the crest of a sloping ridge at 2.8 miles.

Follow cairns and hike more gradually for 0.2 miles to the Baldface Knob Trail junction on the left. Continue angling steadily up the fully exposed ridge and stay on the marked trail to avoid damage to alpine vegetation. At 3.4 miles, arrive at the summit of South Baldface, elevation 3,570

Hikers ascend the steep ledges of South Baldface.

feet, identified by a large cairn and wooden sign. Look east to savor breathtaking views of the Wild River Valley below, the Carter Mountain Range looming beyond, and Mount Washington towering ominously above them on the horizon line.

Turn right on the broad, plateaulike summit and descend northeast into a stunted spruce growth. Climb up onto a substantial rock shelf at 3.8 miles, then drop 0.2 miles to the col between North and South Baldface. Climb abruptly to the top of North Baldface, elevation 3,610 feet, at 4.4 miles. This alpine summit provides 360-degree views, including the Presidentials to the northwest and the Mahoosuc Range due north.

Descend precipitously on ragged granite shelves and boulders to a sizable ledge at 4.8 miles. Glance south for compelling glimpses of the stunning cliffs of South Baldface. Resume dropping steadily to a depression where Bicknell Ridge Trail departs on the right at 5.2 miles. Bicknell Ridge Trail allows for another means of egress. However, it deprives hikers of the opportunity to visit scenic Eagle Crag and only minimally shortens the trip, so I don't recommend it.

Hike up a mild gradient and reach a significant trail junction at 5.4 miles. Eagle Link Trail descends west into the Wild River Valley. Meader Ridge Trail leaves northeast, traverses Eagle

Crag, and continues to Mount Meader, while Baldface Circle Trail turns right and departs to the southeast. Take a few minutes and hike 0.1 mile to Eagle Crag and the last opportunity for expansive views on the trip. From the rocky knob, most of the Baldface ridge is visible to the southeast, and picturesque Cold River Valley lies farther down in the east.

Return to Baldface Circle Trail and scramble down a steep boulder and rock-surfaced path in a thickly forested area for 0.8 miles. At 6.2 miles, the gradient moderates but persists steadily downward as the trail becomes more hard-packed dirt and reaches the Bicknell Ridge Trail junction on the right at 7.6 miles. Skirt along Charles Brook, then cross it, and arrive at the Circle Trail junction at 8 miles. *Note:* Charles Brook may not be passable during periods of high water.

On the left near the junction is a side trail that leads 0.1 mile to a small, unique waterfall with calm water below called Emerald Pool. On hot summer days, this location provides the perfect opportunity for a cool, refreshing swim. From the junction, hike easily for 0.7 miles to the parking area.

Hiking options abound in Evans Notch. From the trailhead parking area, paths lead east for easy hikes to Deer Hill and Little Deer Hill. Two miles farther north on NH 113 at Brickett Place Trailhead, more demanding hikes begin for Speckled, East Royce, and West Royce mountains. Still farther north on NH 113 is the trailhead for Caribou Mountain.

Weather and Lodging

Adverse weather during any season is always a risk on the Baldface Loop Trip. Hikers will experience almost continuous exposure to the elements for about 4 miles beginning on the steep ledges of South Baldface and ending on Eagle Crag. Gusty winds are particularly common. Always carry sufficient protective clothing and gear to address potential weather hazards. The best time for the Baldface climb is summer and early fall. Avoid ascents of the South Baldface ledges when they are wet or icy.

Prior to planning a Baldface Loop Trip, obtain a reliable mountain weather forecast. The best option is the Mount Washington Observatory summit forecast, which is available on their Web site at www.mountwashington.org. Only about 15 miles west, Mount Washington should be an indicator of possible conditions on the Baldface Ridge. However, because Mount Washington is almost 3,000 feet higher, its weather is generally more severe.

Numerous resorts, hotels, motels, and bed-and-breakfasts are available in the North Conway area about 30 miles away. Camping is an option at Basin and Cold River campgrounds in Evans Notch on a first-come, first-serve basis. Hikers can also reserve lodging at the nearby Appalachian Mountain Club (AMC) Cold River Camp through their Web site at www.outdoors.org. North Conway is a shopping destination, and several businesses specialize in hiking, climbing, mountaineering, and camping clothing and equipment.

24   *Goose Eye Mountain*

GOOSE EYE TRAIL

GPS Trailhead Coordinates

UTM Zone (WGS 84)	19T
Easting	0337611.8
Northing	4930344.3
Latitude	N 44° 30'38.59"
Longitude	W 71° 02'32.89"

🚶 Key Information

LENGTH 5.84 miles

ROUTE CONFIGURATION Out-and-back

DIFFICULTY Moderate

ELEVATION GAIN 2,223 feet

SCENERY Exceptional views of the Mahoosuc Mountain Range in eastern New Hampshire and western Maine

EXPOSURE Some exposure to the elements at higher elevations

TRAIL TRAFFIC Light to moderate

TRAIL SURFACE Hard-packed dirt and rock, with ledge scrambling near the summit

CLIMBING TIME 6 hours

DRIVING DISTANCE Approximately 117 miles from the junction of Interstates 93 and 89 in Concord, NH

ACCESS No fees or permits required

MAPS USGS Quadrangles for Success Pond and Old Speck

FACILITIES None

WATER REQUIREMENT 2 quarts per person recommended

DOGS ALLOWED Yes

ELEVATION PROFILE

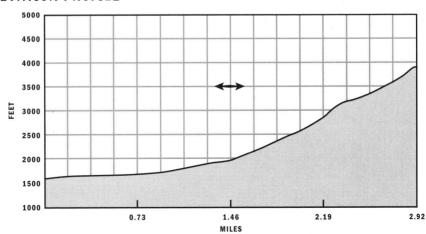

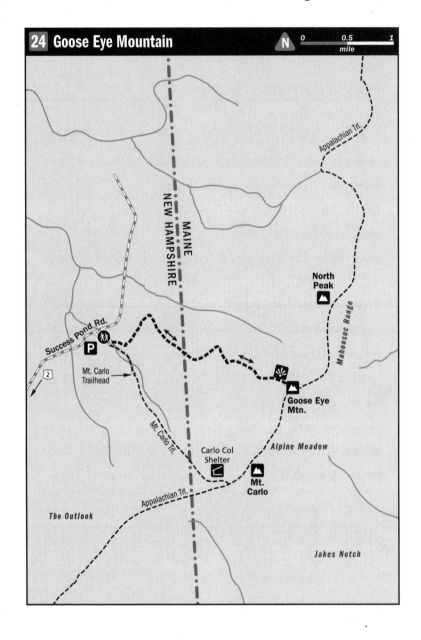

24 Goose Eye Mountain

N 0   0.5   1
mile

Appalachian Trl.

MAINE
NEW HAMPSHIRE

North
Peak

Mahoosuc Range

Success Pond Rd.

P

2

Mt. Carlo
Trailhead

Mt. Carlo Trl.

Goose Eye
Mtn.

Carlo Col
Shelter

Alpine Meadow

Appalachian Trl.

Mt.
Carlo

The Outlook

Jakes Notch

Directions

From the intersection of I-93 and I-89 in Concord, NH, follow I-93 north 76.9 miles to the exit for NH 3 in Franconia. Go straight on NH 3 10.4 miles to an intersection with US 302 in Twin Mountain. Cross US 302 and continue 2 miles on NH 3. In Carroll, turn right on NH 115 and drive 9 miles to US 2 in Jefferson. Turn right and drive 13 miles east to the junction with NH 16 in Gorham. Turn left on NH 16 and drive 5 miles to Unity Street on the right in Berlin. Go 0.8 miles on Unity Street to Coos Street. Remain on Coos Street 0.1 mile to Hutchins Street. Continue 0.5 miles to Dutil Street on the right. Turn right and go 0.2 miles to Success Pond Road. Follow Success Pond Road, a gravel logging road in fair condition, 8.8 miles to a dirt road on the right with a sign for the Goose Eye Trail. A small parking area is on the immediate left.

In Brief

Goose Eye Mountain is in the Mahoosuc Mountain Range, on the border between Maine and New Hampshire. The alpine summit provides phenomenal 360-degree views of the Mahoosuc Mountain Range and the White Mountains of New Hampshire. Some rock and ledge scrambling is required near the top.

Description

From the parking area, walk up the dirt road 80 yards and turn left opposite a cairn on the right side of the road. Enter a dense forest of mixed hardwood and conifer next to a partially obstructed Goose Eye Trail sign attached to a tree, then drop down on stone steps to a boardwalk in a low and damp shaded area. Hike easily for 0.3 miles to a wide stream. Rock-hop across and continue to a dirt road at 0.5 miles. Turn left on the dirt road and go 0.1 mile past two cairns on the left to a trail sign on the right for the AMC Goose Eye Trail.

Turn right on a narrow, hard-packed dirt path with some loose rocks and exposed tree roots. Continue hiking easily while enjoying sporadic views of the distinct alpine Goose Eye Mountain crest. Traverse an old logging road near the Maine/New Hampshire border at 1.25 miles and begin climbing more steadily in an extensive stand of new-growth maples on a good, solid dirt surface. At 1.8 miles, encounter steeper, rockier trail conditions in a mixed white-birch-and-spruce forest.

Ascend the north shoulder of the mountain on an attenuated, precipitous route in thick overhanging spruce. Reach the top of the shoulder at 2.4 miles and glance back to the north for unsurpassed views of Success Pond and the mountains of southern Quebec. Hike gradually for 0.1 mile on a firm, conifer needle–covered path in a thick growth of evergreens and then enter a damp, shaded area with some boulder scrambling. At 2.6 miles, clamber up long, sloping ledges in a substantially exposed environment.

Reach a cliff face at 2.8 miles. Angle left, scale large boulders, and emerge above tree line. Here you encounter breathtaking views in all directions. Carefully climb a precipitous slanted ledge to a large bulbous rock, the Goose Eye Mountain high point, at 2.9 miles. A wooden "Goose Eye Trail" sign is posted nearby.

Hikers on summit of Goose Eye Mountain

From the summit, savor unparalleled 360-degree views. The Mahoosuc Mountain Range extends north and south, with Old Speck and the Baldpates looming beyond in the north, and the towering pinnacles of the White Mountains commanding the southern horizon. Peaks of Evans Notch and the Oxford Hills rise up in the east, while panoramic vistas of the mountains of Quebec can be enjoyed north and west. Cautiously descend the abrupt summit ledges and return to the trailhead near Success Pond Road.

The Mahoosucs provide an abundance of hiking opportunities. The Success, Notch, and Speck Pond trails climb to the ridge from Success Pond Road. The newly constructed Wright Trail ascends to Goose Eye from the east, and the Appalachian Trail traverses the entire range.

A Goose Eye Mountain loop hike is possible. This option entails negotiating a particularly rugged section of the Appalachian Trail and ascending Mount Carlo, elevation 3,565 feet. The loop adds more than 1 mile to the trek and increases the difficulty level from moderate to strenuous. Do not attempt it unless sufficient daylight remains and all members of the group are prepared for intensified physical demands.

To complete the loop from the summit of Goose Eye Mountain, hike east on an exposed narrow ridge for 0.1 mile to a junction with the Appalachian Trail, marked with a large wooden sign. Turn right (south) and descend steadily on a boulder-strewn path, following white blazes. Arch down a wooden ladder attached to a near-vertical 25-foot cliff and negotiate a steep section of rocks and ledges to a mountain meadow. Traverse the meadow, drop below tree line on precipitous ledges in mountain scrub, and reach the saddle between Goose Eye and Carlo at 3.6 miles.

Follow a boardwalk through a boggy heath in the saddle and ascend a steep rock-and-ledge path in a stand of stunted spruce growth for 0.1 mile until you reach a small alpine meadow on the north slope of Mount Carlo. Face north for excellent views of Goose Eye Mountain's unmistakable alpine crown. Persevere up a slanted ledge and over three minor peaks to Mount Carlo summit, marked with a cairn and a USGS marker embedded in stone at 4.1 miles.

Negotiate a section of boardwalk in an open area with views south and drop down precipitous ledges to Carlo Col Trail junction on the right at 4.4 miles. Turn right and continue steadily downward on a heavily rooted, rock-strewn surface in a mixed-hardwood-and-conifer forest to Carlo Col Shelter junction on the right at 4.7 miles. To visit the shelter, scale a steep bank to a sturdy, open-faced log hut with a primitive toilet and tent platforms nearby.

Recommence descending the Carlo Col Trail cautiously on a rocky, damp, and slippery section of path, following blue blazes for 0.1 mile. Reach drier ground and continue dropping to a major stream crossing at 5 miles. Persist down on a hard-packed dirt-and-rock surface with significant tree-root exposure in a predominantly hardwood forest to another consequential stream traverse at 5.7 miles.

Just beyond, arrive at an extensively logged area with fields of slash and overturned topsoil. Carefully follow the remains of the hiking trail while watching for blue blazes on rocks and stumps that fall off the treeless ridge to the left (west). Reenter a hardwood forest and hike easily down a good dirt path parallel to a boulder-filled stream and emerge on a gravel road next to a sign for Carlo Col Trail at 6.3 miles. Turn right and complete the loop by walking down the road for 0.7 miles past the Goose Eye trailhead to the Success Pond Road parking area.

Weather and Lodging

Exposure to the elements on the out-and-back hike to the summit of Goose Eye Mountain is limited to the last 0.2 miles. However, gusty winds, particularly from the north, can be especially harsh, and climbers should be prepared with adequate protective clothing and gear. Those who decide to challenge the loop trip should be prepared for extended exposure to sun, rain, cold, and heavy winds on the Appalachian Trail portion of the trek. Summer and fall are the best seasons for a hike on Goose Eye Mountain. Stream crossings may be hazardous during the spring or after heavy rains.

A few motels and bed-and-breakfasts are available in Berlin. The best options are further south on NH 16 in Gorham, where numerous hotels, motels, and bed-and-breakfasts are located. A good camping choice is Moose Brook State Park on US 2 in Gorham. Several businesses in Gorham retail hiking, climbing, and mountaineering equipment, clothing, and gear.

25   *Potash Mountain*
DOWNES BROOK AND POTASH MOUNTAIN TRAILS

GPS Trailhead Coordinates

UTM Zone (WGS 84)	19T
Easting	0309954.7
Northing	4873967.3
Latitude	N 43° 59'46.61"
Longitude	W 71° 22'10.83"

🚶 Key Information

LENGTH 4.3 miles

ROUTE CONFIGURATION Out-and-back

DIFFICULTY Easy

ELEVATION GAIN Approximately 1,400 feet

SCENERY Outstanding views of the southern White Mountains from the summit

EXPOSURE Some exposure to the elements at higher elevations

TRAIL TRAFFIC Moderate

TRAIL SURFACE Hard-packed dirt and rock with some steep ledge scrambling, particularly near the summit

CLIMBING TIME 4 hours

DRIVING DISTANCE Approximately 88 miles from the junction of Interstate 95 and NH 16 in Portsmouth, NH

ACCESS A day-use parking fee is required

MAPS USGS Quadrangles for Mount Tripyramid and Mount Chocorua

FACILITIES None

WATER REQUIREMENT 1.5 quarts per person recommended

DOGS ALLOWED Yes

ELEVATION PROFILE

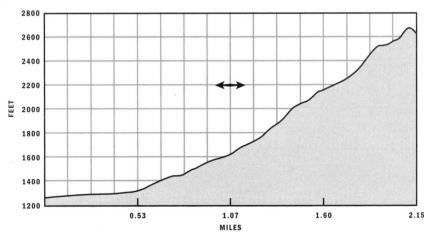

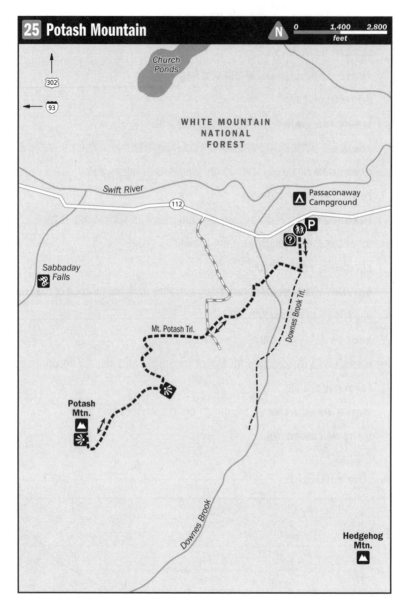

A hiker crosses Downes Brook at low water on the Potash Mountain Trail.

Directions

From the intersection of I-95 and NH 16 in Portsmouth, NH, follow NH 16 (which is also NH 4 and the Spaulding Turnpike, initially) 74.2 miles to NH 112 (Kancamagus Highway) on the left in Conway. Turn left and drive 13.6 miles on scenic Kancamagus Highway to a parking area on the left, which is almost directly opposite the Passaconaway Campground. The trailhead is at the far end of the parking area and to the left of a self-service pay station.

In Brief

Located just south of the Kancamagus Highway in north-central New Hampshire, the summit of Potash Mountain, elevation 2,669 feet, provides outstanding 360-degree vistas of the southern White Mountains. Open ledges on its southeast face offer spectacular views of Hedgehog and Passaconaway mountains and beyond.

Views of the southern White Mountains from the summit of Potash Mountain

Description

From Downes Brook trailhead, walk easily 100 yards on an excellent gravel footpath past an information kiosk on the right and a side trail to Hedgehog Mountain on the left. Angle right and continue hiking on a good hard-packed dirt trail in a mixed hardwood and conifer forest for 0.2 miles to the Potash Mountain Trail junction on the right.

Turn right onto Potash Mountain Trail, follow yellow blazes, and go 0.1 mile on a dirt-and-rock surface to Downes Brook at 0.3 miles. Exercise added caution while negotiating the often-slippery rocks on this wide stream traverse. Do not attempt this crossing when the water is high or a safe route is not obvious.

Hike carefully to avoid considerable tree-root exposure while ascending steadily for 0.5 miles. Cross an old logging road at 0.8 miles and clamber up a steep bank. Reenter the forest where a medium-size cairn marks the trail and continue on rocky terrain. Intersect a dry streambed to a stand of tall spruce trees at 1 mile. Recommence climbing higher on sharply inclined, heavily rooted granite switchbacks to an open ledge facing east at 1.5 miles. Take time to savor exceptional views of Downes Brook Valley below, with Hedgehog Mountain and massive Mount Passaconaway rising beyond.

Skirt the edge of the attenuated ledge, hike through a thick spruce growth, and traverse another exposed ledge. Clamber up a steep, boulder-strewn surface for 0.2 miles, angle more gradually in a southwesterly direction, and arrive at a viewpoint facing a long slide on the northwest slope of Mount Passaconaway at 1.9 miles. Scale an extended succession of up-sloping ledges in patchy scrub to the summit at 2.13 miles.

The summit area provides outstanding panoramic vistas. Numerous peaks are visible to the north and west along Kancamagus Highway and beyond. Surveying the horizon counterclockwise from north to southwest, you'll take in Mount Carrigain, the Hancocks, the Bonds, the Osceolas, and the Tripyramids. Farther northwest, spectacular Franconia Ridge dominates in the distance. This is an ideal location for an extended respite or a leisurely picnic lunch. Carefully and deliberately descend the steep, protracted summit ledges and return to the Kancamagus Highway parking lot.

Hiking options abound all along Kancamagus Highway. Nearly 20 trails leave the road, leading both north and south. They connect with dozens more and offer a variety of options, including easy day hikes, arduous ascents to 4,000-foot summits, and extended backpacking trips.

History, Weather, and Lodging

Named for a famous Native American warrior who fought during the French and Indian Wars, Kancamagus Highway, which provides access to Potash Mountain, is one of the most scenic roads in New England. Beginning in Conway in the east, it travels west 35 miles through the heart of the White Mountains to Lincoln. Built in 1959, it parallels two popular whitewater rivers, the Swift and Pemigewasset, in a spectacular alpine environment. It passes waterfalls and raging torrents in the shadows of towering summits and climbs dramatically through picturesque Kancamagus Pass at an elevation of almost 3,000 feet. Prior to its construction, this marvelous mountain wilderness was inaccessible to all but a few.

Most of the climb to the summit of Potash Mountain is below tree line with little exposure to the elements. Downes Brook may be dangerous or impassable during periods of high water; avoid it in spring or after heavy rains. The best time for a hike to the summit is in fall, when the stream is usually low and autumn foliage is at its peak.

Several National Forest Service first-come, first-serve campgrounds are available along Kancamagus Highway. The most convenient to Potash Mountain is Passaconaway Campground, which is directly across the road from the trailhead. A multitude of resorts, hotels, motels, and bed-and-breakfasts are located in nearby North Conway and Lincoln. Both communities have several retailers that specialize in hiking, climbing, and mountaineering gear, clothing, and supplies.

26 MOUNT TOM

RHODE ISLAND

26 *Mount Tom*

MOUNT TOM TRAIL

GPS Trailhead Coordinates

UTM Zone (WGS 84)	19T
Easting	0273041.9
Northing	4605714.1
Latitude	N 41° 34'22.43"
Longitude	W 71° 43'17.97"

🥾 Key Information

LENGTH 4.58 miles

ROUTE CONFIGURATION Out-and-back

DIFFICULTY Easy

ELEVATION GAIN 294 feet

SCENERY Excellent views of southwestern Rhode Island and eastern Connecticut landscape from Mount Tom Cliffs

EXPOSURE Negligible

TRAIL TRAFFIC Moderate

TRAIL SURFACE Hard-packed dirt and rock, some ledge

CLIMBING TIME 3 hours

DRIVING DISTANCE Approximately 20 miles from the junction of Interstates 95 and 295 in Warwick, RI

ACCESS No fees or permits required

MAPS USGS Quadrangle for Hope Valley

FACILITIES None

WATER REQUIREMENT 1 quart per person recommended

DOGS ALLOWED Yes

ELEVATION PROFILE

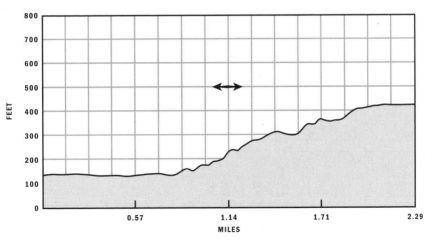

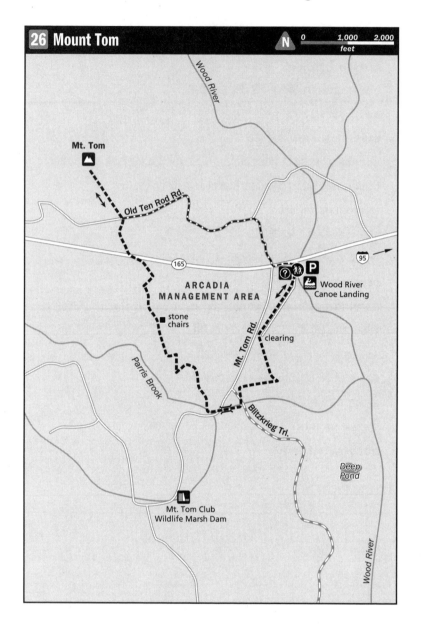

Directions

From the intersection of I-95 and I-295 in Warwick, RI, follow I-95 south 15 miles to RI 102, Exit 5. Turn left on RI 102 and go 0.5 miles to RI 3. Turn right and drive 0.5 miles south to RI 165. Go west 2.5 miles on RI 165 to a parking area on the left marked with a sign "Arcadia Management Area Check Station and Wood River Canoe Access." Drive straight into the parking area past a red Quonset hut and information kiosk on the left; park on the right. The trailhead is located in the right rear corner of the parking area.

In Brief

Located in southwestern Rhode Island a few miles from the Connecticut border, Mount Tom is part of the Arcadia Wildlife Management Area. Mount Tom Trail to the summit, elevation 426 feet, is an easy hike with minimal rock and ledge scrambling. A section of the trail known as Mount Tom Cliffs provides expansive views of the surrounding landscape.

Description

From the right rear corner of the parking area, walk south 50 yards through an opening in a stand of tall pines until you reach two five-foot-tall wooden posts where a Mount Tom Trail sign is attached to a tree on the left. Go between the posts and follow white blazes on a flat dirt road in a sparse, predominantly pine forest to a clearing with a wood-chip surface at 0.3 miles. Motorized traffic is banned on the road.

Several trails or roads exit from the clearing and can cause confusion. Turn left and follow white blazes on a hard-packed-dirt footpath 0.3 miles to a gravel road. Turn left and walk 50 yards on the road to a narrow opening on the right. Reenter the forest next to a partially obstructed Mount Tom Trail sign in dense mixed vegetation consisting of tall ferns, hardwoods, and conifers. Hike parallel to a small brook on a firm dirt-and-grass surface 0.3 miles to a paved road at 0.9 miles.

Turn left on the paved road and go 20 yards to a wooden Mount Tom Trail sign on the right. Recommence hiking in a wooded area, gaining moderate elevation on a rocky path. At 1 mile, large boulders on a gentle ridge constitute the beginning of the Mount Tom Cliffs. Negotiate a boulder-strewn trail in a thin stand of hardwoods with sporadic views in all directions to a scenic elevated location with three chairs built of stone slabs. Stop to rest and enjoy the views in this picturesque setting.

Drop down briefly and then climb gradually on a rock-and-hard-packed-dirt trail. At 1.75 miles, arrive at a large boulder on the right that affords excellent views of the rolling hills of southern Rhode Island to the east. Persist on a rocky surface to RI 165 at 1.9 miles.

Angle left and carefully cross busy RI 165 toward a white blaze painted on a large rock. Reenter the forest next to a Mount Tom Trail sign in a stand of small maple trees and ascend on a surface of loose rocks and gravel. Reach a good and solid, almost level earthen trail and continue to Old Ten Rod Road Trail junction on the right at 2 miles.

A hiker on the Mount Tom Trail

Turn left onto Mount Tom Trail. Follow this excellent route in a predominantly hardwood forest 0.3 miles to the summit at 2.3 miles. No summit marker exists, and the true high point is not obvious, but an old, inconspicuous path leads right at this spot. If you reach an unmarked trail junction with an ancient stonewall on the left, you are 0.2 miles beyond the high point. From the summit, descend gradually to return to RI 165, traverse Mount Tom Cliffs, and return to the Arcadia Management Station trailhead.

A shorter loop trip is possible. From the summit, return 0.3 miles to Old Ten Rod Road Trail junction on the left. Turn left on a good, wide surface and hike southeast 1.25 miles to RI 165. Hike 100 yards east on RI 165, cross the road, and arrive at the entrance to Arcadia Management Station. Starting a hike on RI 165 at mile 1.9 is not recommended due to insufficient space for safe parking.

Arcadia Wildlife Management Area has an extensive trail system with a multitude of hiking options. The 6-mile Arcadia Trail begins on the Arcadia Road about a mile east of the Mount Tom trailhead. Breakheart and John Hudson trails access Breakheart Pond east of

Mount Tom, and Escoheag Trail connects with the northern terminus of the Mount Tom Trail after departing from Escoheag Road west of Mount Tom.

History, Weather, and Lodging

Arcadia Wildlife Management Area is an outdoor recreational paradise consisting of more than 14,000 forested acres. More than 30 miles of hiking trails are maintained by the Narragansett Chapter of the Appalachian Mountain Club and the Rhode Island Department of Environmental Management. The area is also a popular destination for backpackers, equestrians, and mountain bikers. Canoeists and kayakers challenge the Class I and II rapids of Wood River, which intersects the wilderness area.

Virtually all of the Mount Tom Trail is below tree line, with little exposure to the elements. Spring, summer, and fall are all good times for a hike on Mount Tom or in the wilderness area. Mount Tom Trail is a popular hike during peak autumn foliage, which normally occurs during late September or early October.

Mount Tom is situated in a rural area of Rhode Island with limited lodging options. Some motels and hotels can be found in the nearby towns of Wyoming, Rockville, and Hopkinton. The best selections for lodging are located in Warwick, RI, or Norwich and New London, CT. A good camping alternative is Hopeville Pond State Park, about 15 miles west in Griswold, CT.

VERMONT

27   *Camel's Hump*
BURROWS AND LONG TRAILS

GPS Trailhead Coordinates
UTM Zone (WGS 84)	18T
Easting	0666843.7
Northing	4907668.2
Latitude	N 44° 18'18.49"
Longitude	W 72° 54'28.29"

𝕩𝕩 Key Information

LENGTH 4.72 miles

ROUTE CONFIGURATION Out-and-back

DIFFICULTY Easy to moderate

ELEVATION GAIN Less than 2,300 feet

SCENERY Outstanding 360-degree views of northern Vermont from The Hump

EXPOSURE Minimal exposure to the elements, limited to the summit area

TRAIL TRAFFIC Moderate

TRAIL SURFACE Hard-packed dirt and rock with some ledge scrambling at higher elevations

CLIMBING TIME 4.5 hours

DRIVING DISTANCE Approximately 15 miles from the junction of Interstate 89 and US 2 near Burlington, VT

ACCESS No fees or permits required

MAPS USGS Quadrangle for Huntington

FACILITIES None

WATER REQUIREMENT 1.5 quarts per person recommended

DOGS ALLOWED Yes

ELEVATION PROFILE

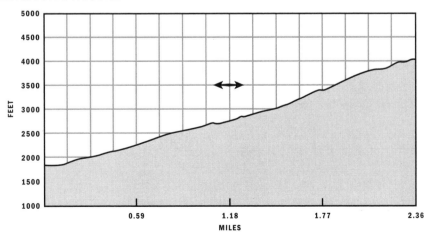

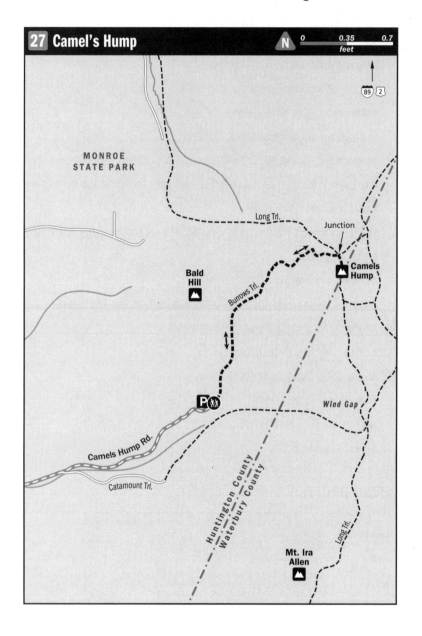

27 Camel's Hump

N   0   0.35   0.7
feet

89 2

MONROE
STATE PARK

Long Trl.

Junction

Bald
Hill

Burrows Trl.

Camels
Hump

P ☂

Wind Gap

Camels Hump Rd.

Catamount Trl.

Huntington County
Waterbury County

Long Trl.

Mt. Ira
Allen

Directions

From the intersection of I-89 and US 2 at Exit 11 5 miles east of Burlington, VT, follow US 2 east 2.1 miles to Bridge Street on the right in Richmond. Turn right and go 0.4 miles to Huntington Road on the right. Continue on the Huntington Road 8.9 miles through Huntington to Camel's Hump Road on the left in Huntington Center. Turn left on a good dirt road and drive 3.6 miles to a parking area at the Burrows Trailhead, where the road ends. The trailhead is at the far end of the parking area.

In Brief

Located in northwestern Vermont, the barren, rounded ridge of Camel's Hump, elevation 4,086 feet, is one of the most distinctive landmarks in the Green Mountains. The summit area is one of only two alpine zones in Vermont and provides splendid 360-degree views of the Green Mountains and Adirondacks of northeastern New York. The Burrows and Long trails hike to the top is easy to moderate in difficulty and provides one of the least demanding climbs to a 4,000-foot summit in New England. Much of the surface is hard-packed dirt and rock, well marked and in fair condition, with some trail erosion. Expect a modest amount of rock and ledge scrambling at higher elevations. Most of the hike is below tree line, with minimal exposure to the elements.

Description

Walk through a narrow, unmarked opening in thick vegetation at the eastern end of the parking area and cross two short bridges to arrive at the Burrows trailhead, where there is an information kiosk and trail sign. The kiosk has a large map of the environs and a sign-in register. Sign in and hike steadily on a trail of hard-packed dirt and rock, with considerable tree-root exposure in a forest of mixed hardwood and conifer.

Continue ascending under a canopy of tall elm and maple trees for 1 mile. At 1.2 miles, the character of the woodland changes to a white-birch-and-spruce forest. Look east for glimpses of The Hump towering above. Scramble steeply up a boulder-strewn section of trail at 1.7 miles, then drop into a slight depression.

Recommence climbing in a dense, stunted spruce growth and arrive at a flat, open area, elevation 3,820 feet, at 2.1 miles. Formerly the site of a lodge built in the 19th century that subsequently burned, it is now a major trail junction. The Long Trail traverses north and south at this intersection, and the Monroe Trail descends to the southeast; camping is prohibited.

Follow the Long Trail south and reenter the spruce forest. Clamber steeply up a rugged rock and ledge–surfaced path with sporadic views to the west, and emerge above tree line in an arctic alpine zone at 2.2 miles. Pause and appreciate outstanding panoramic vistas of the Adirondacks of northeastern New York. Heed signs warning of a fragile alpine ecosystem and continue climbing while cautiously following cairns and white trail blazes. Scramble up the granite summit dome and reach the top, which is identified with a USGS marker embedded in stone at 2.36 miles.

A hiker ascends the summit cone on Camel's Hump.

The summit offers magnificent views in all directions. Commanding Mount Mansfield dominates the north, while Mount Washington and the White Mountains of New Hampshire are often visible in the east. The Green Mountains extend to the south, and much of Lake Champlain can be seen in the west, with Mount Marcy and the lofty peaks of the Adirondacks recognizable beyond. The massive boulders provide shelter from any winds for a prolonged visit and picnic lunch while you benefit from the incredible scenery. Carefully descend the precipitous ledges north on the Long Trail, rejoin the Burrows Trail, and return to the parking area.

Camel's Hump is one of the most popular hiking destinations in New England, with thousands of day-hikers and backpackers visiting each year. Trails lead to the summit or connect with the Long Trail from all directions. The Dean Trail leads south from US 2, and the Monroe Trail approaches from the east. These, along with the Burrows Trail from the west and others, all join the Long Trail, which in turn traverses Camel's Hump north and south.

History, Weather, and Lodging

Prehistoric Native Americans lived in the shadows of Camel's Hump for thousands of years. French Explorer Samuel de Champlain reconnoitered the region early in the 17th century and reputedly named the mountain Le Lion Couchant (the Crouching Lion). Subsequently known as Camel's Rump, it was finally assigned the more polite moniker of Camel's Hump in the 19th century.

Most of the climb is located below tree line and sheltered from the elements. Expect limited exposure to sun, rain, cold, and particularly gusty winds in the summit area. The best time for a hike on the Burrows Trail to the top is spring, summer, or fall.

The peak was originally gifted to the State of Vermont in 1909 and formally designated as a forest reserve in 1969. Camel's Hump State Park, consisting of approximately 20,000 acres, was created in 1991. The Green Mountain Club maintains several shelters and lodges in the park. Gorham Lodge is located 0.7 miles north of the summit on the Long Trail, and Montclair Glen Lodge 0.9 miles south. Primitive camping is allowed at lower elevations, and tent sites are available at Hump Brook Tenting Area. For additional information, access the Vermont State Parks Web site at www.vtstateparks.com or call (802) 879-6565.

A few bed-and-breakfasts are located in Huntington and Richmond. Numerous motels, hotels, and bed-and-breakfasts are available in Burlington, where several businesses retail hiking, climbing, and camping gear and equipment. Lodging can also be obtained farther east in Waterbury and Montpelier. Little River State Park in Waterbury has a large campground with more than 80 sites. Access the Vermont State Parks Web site or call (802) 244-7103 for additional information.

28   *Equinox Mountain*
BLUE SUMMIT TRAIL

GPS Trailhead Coordinates

UTM Zone (WGS 84)	18T
Easting	0655857.8
Northing	4780457.1
Latitude	N 43° 09'46.17"
Longitude	W 73° 04'56.62"

👭 Key Information

LENGTH 5.2 miles

ROUTE CONFIGURATION Out-and-back

DIFFICULTY Moderate

ELEVATION GAIN Exceeds 2,700 feet

SCENERY Expansive views of south-central Vermont and eastern New York from the summit

EXPOSURE Minimal exposure to the elements

TRAIL TRAFFIC Moderate

TRAIL SURFACE Primarily hard-packed dirt and rock

CLIMBING TIME 5 hours

DRIVING DISTANCE Approximately 70 miles from the junction of Interstate 91 and VT 9 in Brattleboro, VT

ACCESS No fees or permits required

MAPS USGS Quadrangle for Manchester

FACILITIES None

WATER REQUIREMENT 1.5 quarts per person recommended

DOGS ALLOWED Yes

ELEVATION PROFILE

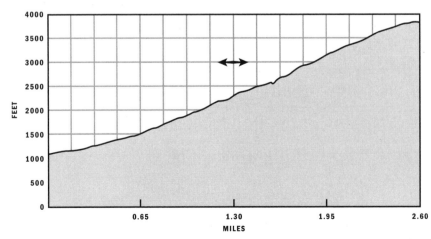

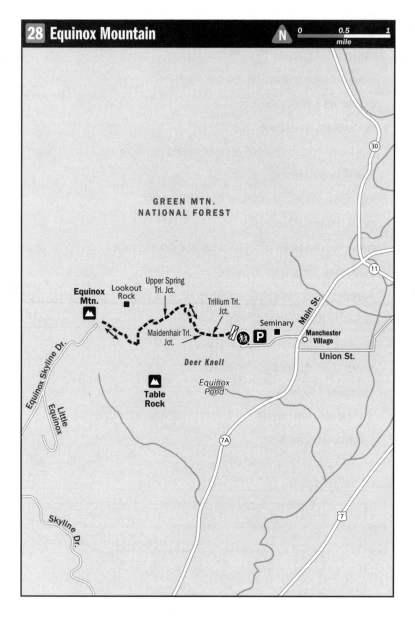

28 Equinox Mountain
N
0   0.5   1
mile

GREEN MTN.
NATIONAL FOREST

Upper Spring
Trl. Jct.

Equinox
Mtn.

Lookout
Rock

Trillium Trl.
Jct.

Maidenhair Trl.
Jct.

Seminary

Manchester
Village

Union St.

Main St.

Equinox Skyline Dr.

Little Equinox

Deer Knoll

Equinox Pond

Table
Rock

Skyline Dr.

7A

30

11

7

A hiker on the Blue Summit Trail

Directions

From the intersection of I-91 and VT 9 in Brattleboro, VT, follow VT 9 west 39 miles to US 7 in Bennington. Drive north on US 7 26 miles to Exit 4 (VT 11) in Manchester. Follow VT 11 west toward Manchester Village for 0.9 miles. Turn left on Richville Road and go 0.9 miles. Turn right on Union Street and drive 0.9 miles. Turn right on Main Street and then immediately turn left onto Seminary Avenue. Drive 0.2 miles, bear left onto Prospect Street, and then go 0.1 mile. Turn right on West Union Street and go 0.2 miles to an unmarked, crushed-rock parking area on the right. The trail is a gravel road leaving from the northwest corner of the parking area.

In Brief

Located near the New York border just a few miles from Bennington, VT, and Albany, NY, Equinox Mountain, elevation 3,833 feet, is one of the most prominent peaks in southwestern Vermont. The entire hike is below tree line with minimal exposure to the elements. The

Taking a break on the Blue Summit Trail

summit area provides expansive views to the north and east of south-central Vermont and eastern New York.

Description

From the parking area, follow a gravel road northwest past a concrete cistern in a small, open field on the left for 0.1 mile to a steel gate. Go around the gate and continue on the road in a mixed hardwood, old-growth forest, passing junctions for Flatlanders and Snicket trails on the left. At 0.3 miles, arrive at the trailhead for Blue Summit Trail at a fork in the road. Bear left (west) and carefully follow the route marked with blue blazes, as there are several trails in this area.

Hike easily on a wide, well-marked path in excellent condition, intersecting with the Trillium Trail at 0.4 miles and Maidenhair Trail at 0.6 miles. Pass a cabin on the left and ascend the unrelenting path into a canopy of overhanging hardwoods on the east slope of the mountain for 0.6 miles.

At 1.2 miles, level off for 150 yards, skirt the edge of a severe incline for 0.2 miles, and reach a junction with Upper Spring Trail on the left at 1.5 miles. A spring tumbles precipitously down the east side of the mountain 100 yards south on the Upper Spring Trail. Prior to consumption, treat or purify this or any other water source on Equinox Mountain.

From the Upper Spring Trail junction, turn right, leave the old road, and climb steadily on a narrow, rocky path. At 2 miles, angle sharply to the right onto the east shoulder of the mountain and hike up through a sparse conifer forest with some blowdown. Continue northwesterly, with only occasional blue-blaze trail markings, and enter thick, stunted spruce growth. At 2.4 miles, cross an unmarked trail, hike around a radar tower, and emerge into an opening next to the summit house at 2.6 miles.

The summit house, known as The Inn, is closed so neither shelter nor facilities are available. For the best views, walk around to the north side of The Inn, where you'll enjoy panoramic vistas of the Green Mountains of south-central Vermont and the Adirondacks of eastern New York. Prior to returning to the trailhead in Manchester, take time to study the unique architecture of the summit house, which was designed to withstand heavy winds and a harsh mountain environment.

The Equinox Preservation Trust maintains numerous trails on the eastern slopes of Equinox Mountain. Blue Summit Trail is the only trail to the top. All trails can be accessed from the West Union Street Trailhead. The preserve consists of 850 acres. For more information, visit their Web site at www.equinoxpreservationtrust.org.

History, Weather, and Lodging

There are conflicting explanations as to how Equinox Mountain obtained its name. Some attribute it to an early scientific expedition to the mountain conducted on the equinox, while others believe the name is derived from a Native American word for high mountain that had a similar pronunciation. Regardless, early settlers built farms on its slopes, and hikers and climbers have been ascending to its summit for more than two centuries.

An auto road to the summit, the Equinox Sky Line Drive, was completed and opened in 1947. Shortly thereafter, The Inn was constructed directly over the actual high point to accommodate visitors who motored to the top. The Inn has been closed for several years; however, the gated 5.2-mile auto road is open to the public and operated by The Carthusian Foundation. You can contact them by phone at (802) 362-1115 or access their Web site at www.equinox mountain.com.

Spring, summer, and fall are good times to climb Equinox Mountain. The best time is probably during peak fall foliage, generally late September or early October. Most of the hike is below tree line, so exposure to the elements is minimal. Since there are no significant stream crossings, high-water problems are generally not an issue.

Numerous resorts, hotels, motels, and bed-and-breakfasts are available in Manchester. Campgrounds are located in nearby Peru and Arlington. Manchester is a shopping destination, and several businesses retail hiking, climbing, and camping clothing and equipment.

29 *Mount Mansfield*
EAGLE CUT, SUNSET RIDGE, AND
LONG TRAILS

GPS Trailhead Coordinates

UTM Zone (WGS 84)	18T
Easting	0673496.5
Northing	4934168.6
Latitude	N 44° 31'45.24"
Longitude	W 72° 50'34.68"

🚶 Key Information

LENGTH 5.7 miles

ROUTE CONFIGURATION Out-and-back

DIFFICULTY Moderate

ELEVATION GAIN Approximately 2,600 feet

SCENERY Spectacular views of Lake Champlain, Green Mountains, and eastern New York from Sunset Ridge and summit area

EXPOSURE Considerable exposure to the elements

TRAIL TRAFFIC Moderate to heavy

TRAIL SURFACE Hard-packed dirt and rock at lower elevations and rock and ledge scrambling at higher

CLIMBING TIME 5.5 hours

DRIVING DISTANCE Approximately 20 miles from the junction of Interstate 89 and VT 2A near Burlington, VT

ACCESS Day-use or camping fee required

MAPS USGS Quadrangle for Mount Mansfield

FACILITIES Restrooms at the trailhead

WATER REQUIREMENT 1.5 quarts per person recommended

DOGS ALLOWED Yes

ELEVATION PROFILE

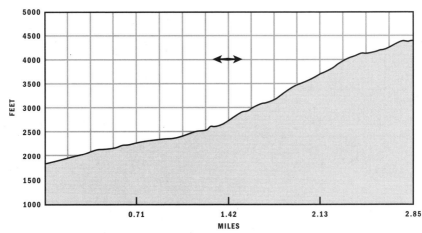

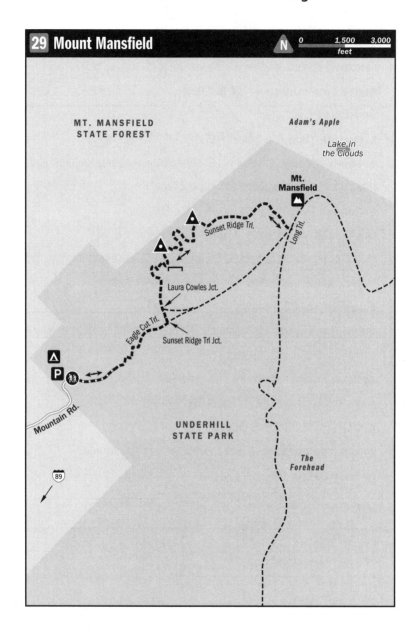

Directions

From the intersection of I-89 and VT 2A 1 mile east of Burlington, VT, go north on VT 2A 3.7 miles to a junction with VT 117 and VT 15 in Essex. Turn right past VT 117 onto VT 15 and drive 9.3 miles to River Road on the right in Underhill. Follow River Road 2.7 miles, then bear left onto North Kruger Road and go 1 mile to Mountain Road. Turn right on Mountain Road and continue 2.4 miles to Underhill State Park. A parking area and campground are located directly across from the ranger's cabin on the right. The trailhead is located at the far end of the parking area, about 30 yards beyond the ranger's cabin.

In Brief

Mount Mansfield, elevation 4,392 feet, is the highest and most frequently climbed peak in Vermont. Located near Lake Champlain in the northwestern corner of the state, the barren summit provides spectacular 360-degree views of the Adirondacks of New York, Lake Champlain, and the Green Mountains of Vermont. Climbing the Sunset Ridge and Long trails out-and-back is moderate in difficulty and the easiest and most scenic route to the top. On this western approach, expect extended exposure to sun, wind, rain, and cold during any season, with considerable rock-and-ledge scrambling, particularly at higher elevations.

Description

From the trailhead, walk up the gated gravel park road 40 yards, turn right, and follow a sign for the Eagle Cut Trail. Enter a mixed-hardwood forest and hike easily on a hard-packed dirt-and-rock path, crossing the park road three times. At 0.4 miles, turn left on the park road and continue past the Youth Camp on the right at 0.6 miles and a cabin on the right just beyond. Reach the Sunset Ridge trailhead at 0.8 miles and sign in at the register on the right.

From Sunset Ridge trailhead, immediately cross three bridges over upper tributaries of turbulent Browns River and continue on a good, hard-packed dirt surface in a mixed-hardwood-and-conifer forest 0.1 mile to the Laura Cowles Trail junction on the right. The Laura Cowles Trail rejoins Sunset Ridge Trail just west of the Long Trail on the summit ridge and allows for an optional loop trip. It is not recommended because it is steep and lacks the almost continuous and magnificent views furnished by Sunset Ridge.

Angle left on Sunset Ridge Trail and continue hiking easily on an obvious, well-maintained but damp path. At 1.2 miles, hike steeply up a rock stairlike stretch past a substantial boulder on the left, cross a short bridge, and arrive at an overlook on the left, where there is a small bench at 1.4 miles. From this vantage point, appreciate excellent views northwest of Lake Champlain and the Adirondacks beyond.

Enter stunted spruce growth and climb steadily on a rocky surface. At 1.6 miles, pass a side trail on the left to the Cantilever Rock Overlook, an easy hike 0.2 miles northwest. Persist upward, scrambling over, around, and between massive boulders and steep ledges, and emerge above tree line at 1.9 miles. Take time to glance back to the west and contemplate the panoramic vista of Lake Champlain. From this point on, expect continuous exposure to the elements.

A hiker descends the Sunset Ridge Trail on Mount Mansfield.

Adverse weather can occur during any season. If you encounter hazardous weather, turn back.

Persevere up the totally exposed ridge, following cairns and blue blazes. In blueberry season (usually during early August), feast on wild blueberries growing along the way. Carefully follow trail markings and heed signs to avoid damaging sensitive alpine vegetation. Reenter thick, patchy spruce growth at 2.3 miles and weave higher in the dense maze to the Laura Cowles Trail junction on the right at 2.65 miles. The more-sheltered Laura Cowles Trail can provide some additional protection from the elements if you encounter severe weather.

Join the Long Trail on the exposed summit ridge, an arctic alpine zone, at 2.7 miles. The Long Trail is a 272-mile-long hiking path that traverses the Green Mountains of Vermont in a north-to-south direction. Follow white blazes and cairns north on the Long Trail over prodigious granite ledges to the summit at 2.86 miles.

From the top, savor truly remarkable 360-degree views. To the west is expansive Lake Champlain, with the Adirondacks of northeastern New York beyond. In the north, the Jay Peaks dominate the horizon, while the White Mountains of New Hampshire are often visible in the east. The summit ridge extends south, seemingly pointing toward the rugged profile of

Camel's Hump presiding over the southern landscape. Enjoy an extended respite in this idyllic mountain paradise prior to returning on the Long Trail and cautiously descending precipitous Sunset Ridge to the Underhill State Park.

An abundance of hiking options exists on Mount Mansfield. Two additional trails depart from the Underhill State Park to the summit. Further to the south, two trails ascend the western slope from Stevensville to the summit ridge. The Long Trail approaches from the south, traverses the summit ridge, and continues east after crossing over the high point. The Nose Dive Trail and others climb the eastern slope from Smuggler's Notch.

History, Weather, and Lodging

Named for the no-longer-existent Town of Mansfield, in which it was located, Mount Mansfield is a prominent part of local Native American legend. Viewed from the east or west, the summit ridge seems to have the profile of a human face. Therefore, several locations are named for facial features, including the nose, lips, forehead, Adam's apple, and chin, which is the high point.

Constructed by the Green Mountain Club early in the 20th century, the Long Trail begins at the Vermont–Massachusetts border and extends north for 272 miles to Canada. It coincides with the Appalachian Trail for about 100 miles and traverses most of the high peaks in Vermont. It has about 70 primitive shelters, including the Taft House on the east side of Mount Mansfield, and is a frequent destination for both backpackers and day-hikers. The Green Mountain Club continues to protect, maintain, and manage the Long Trail.

Adverse weather conditions can occur on Mount Mansfield during any time of year, particularly in the alpine zone. Climbers should obtain a reliable mountain forecast in advance of a planned climb and get a current forecast at the Ranger's Cabin on the day of the hike. Always carry sufficient protective clothing and gear to deal with all weather eventualities. The best time for a climb on Mount Mansfield is late spring through early fall.

Underhill State Park is located in a remote setting; the best option when climbing Mount Mansfield from the west is to camp at the trailhead, which consists of 11 tent sites, six lean-to sites, and a group camping area. For additional information, access the Vermont State Parks Web site at www.vtstateparks.com or call (802) 899-3022. The closest lodging choices are in Burlington, where there are numerous motels, hotels, and bed-and-breakfasts. Several businesses in Burlington retail hiking, climbing, mountaineering, and camping gear and equipment.

30   *Jay Peak*
       LONG TRAIL

GPS Trailhead Coordinates

UTM Zone (WGS 84)	18T
Easting	0696948
Northing	4976057.7
Latitude	N 44° 54'45.76"
Longitude	W 72° 30'16.39"

🥾 Key Information

LENGTH 3.06 miles

ROUTE CONFIGURATION Out-and-back

DIFFICULTY Easy

ELEVATION GAIN 1,579 feet

SCENERY Extensive 360-degree views of northern Vermont and southern Quebec from the summit

EXPOSURE Minimal exposure to the elements

TRAIL TRAFFIC Moderate

TRAIL SURFACE Hard-packed dirt and rock with some ledge scrambling near the summit

CLIMBING TIME 3 hours

DRIVING DISTANCE Approximately 64 miles from the junction of Interstates 91 and 93 in Saint Johnsbury, VT

ACCESS No fees or permits required

MAPS USGS Quadrangle for Jay Peak

FACILITIES None

WATER REQUIREMENT 1 quart per person recommended

DOGS ALLOWED Yes

ELEVATION PROFILE

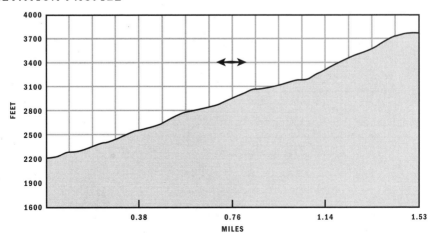

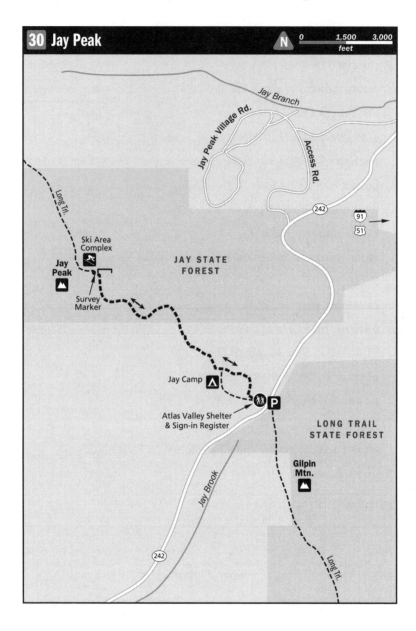

30 Jay Peak

N   0   1,500   3,000
feet

Jay Branch

Jay Peak Village Rd.

Access Rd.

242

91

51

Long Trl.

Ski Area
Complex

**Jay
Peak**

Survey
Marker

JAY STATE
FOREST

Jay Camp

Atlas Valley Shelter
& Sign-in Register

P

LONG TRAIL
STATE FOREST

**Gilpin
Mtn.**

Jay Brook

242

Long Trl.

Hikers approach the summit of Jay Peak from the south.

Directions

From the intersection of I-91 and I-93 in Saint Johnsbury, VT, drive north on I-91 41 miles to VT 191 (Exit 27) in Newport. Go west on VT 191 2.1 miles to the junction with US 5 and VT 105. Turn left onto US 5/VT 105 and travel 4.6 miles to the junction with VT 100. Turn left and go 6.5 miles to VT 101 in Troy. Turn right and drive 3.1 miles to the junction with VT 242 on the left. Follow VT 242 west 6.2 miles to a parking area on the left where the Long Trail intersects. The trailhead for Jay Peak leads north 30 yards west of the parking area on the opposite side of the highway.

In Brief

Jay Peak, elevation 3,770 feet, is situated in northern Vermont near the Canadian border in an area known as the Northeast Kingdom. The Long Trail from VT 242 to the summit is an easy

The summit of Jay Peak

hike with little exposure to the elements. Expect some ledge scrambling and beautiful views on the summit ridge.

Description

From the parking area, cross the road and walk west on VT 242 for 30 yards to the (Long Trail) trailhead, a narrow opening in dense vegetation. Enter a hardwood forest and immediately walk past the Atlas Valley Shelter located on the right. Arrive at a sign-in register adjacent to a spur trail forking left at 0.1 mile. The side trail begins a loop leading south to Jay Camp, an overnight backpackers' shelter operated by the Green Mountain Club.

Sign in and ascend gradually on a narrow, hard-packed dirt and rock surface with considerable tree root exposure. At 0.3 miles, pass the northern terminus of Jay Camp Loop Trail on the left. Continue steadily on a narrow path and follow white blazes in a thick, constricting forest for 0.7 miles to a viewpoint facing southwest at 1.05 miles. From this vantage point, you can observe several peaks of the northern Green Mountains extending south.

At 1.1 miles, angle right and climb steadily on rocky footing in stunted spruce growth to arrive at a small clearing at 1.3 miles. Turn left and clamber up steep ledges adjacent to a Jay Peak Ski Area trail descending a few yards to the right. Continue unrelentingly upward on a boulder-strewn surface and traverse the ski trail at 1.45 miles. Watch for skiers and snowboarders during winter months.

Follow white blazes and scramble up and over a precipitous, rugged granite rock formation in patchy, dense alpine vegetation. Continue climbing cautiously along the attenuated, sloping ridge and savor extensive views in all directions. Arrive at the summit at 1.53 miles.

No sign identifies the actual summit. However, a small USGS marker is embedded in rock at the obvious high point, and a marble bench dedicated to the memory of Richard Meunier is located nearby. The top-of-the-mountain ski complex is 50 yards farther north, slightly below the summit ridge where the tramway enters and exits.

The high point affords magnificent views in all directions. Lush, tree-covered Green Mountains extend north and south as far as the eye can see. On clear days, you can see the White Mountains of New Hampshire in the east and the majestic Adirondacks of New York in the west. The ski area, with numerous trails snaking downward from the summit house, commands the landscape below in the northeast. The top of the mountain is a perfect location for an extended respite or a picnic lunch. Carefully descend the rugged crest and return to the VT 242 trailhead via the Long Trail.

History, Weather, and Lodging

The hike to Jay Peak is part of the Long Trail system known as the Northern Frontier Section and is preserved and supported by the Green Mountain Club (GMC). Frequented by backpackers, this segment of trail begins at VT 58 in Westfield and extends north for about 20 miles to the Canadian border. The GMC maintains the trails and operates five shelters, including the Atlas Valley and Jay Camp Shelters on the south side of Jay Peak.

Expect some exposure to wind, rain, sun, and cold near the top of Jay Peak; however, the balance of the hike is below tree line and sheltered from the direct effects of the elements. Rock and ledge scrambling is required on the narrow, open summit ridge. However, you can avoid much of this section by hiking up and down the steep ski trail beginning and ending at mile 1.45 when the ski area is not operating. Late spring, summer, and early fall are all good times to climb Jay Peak. *Note:* Be sure to obtain a reliable mountain weather forecast prior to your hike, as cold, wintry conditions can arrive prematurely in this northern, mountainous region.

This remote area has limited lodging options nearby. A few choices are available in the vicinity near the entrance to the ski area, and Newport (about 20 miles east of Jay Peak) has several motels, hotels, and bed-and-breakfasts. Private campgrounds are located in Westfield and Morrisville.

APPENDIXES
& INDEX

appendix a: *glossary*

ALPINE   Pertaining to high mountains

ARÊTE   An attenuated mountain ridge

BACKPACKING (V.)   Overnight mountain hiking

BASIN   A large mountain depression where water collects

BLAZE   A painted mark on a tree or rock

BOARDWALK   Low wooden bridge over a damp or swampy area

CAIRN   Mound of stones marking a trail or location

CATARACT   A large waterfall

CIRQUE   The steep upper end of a mountain valley

COL   The low point between two mountains

CRAG   Prominent or overhanging rock

ECOSYSTEM   An ecological community in a physical setting

FJORD   A narrow ocean inlet surrounded by mountains

GORGE   An attenuated, steep valley

HEADWALL   The steep upper end of a mountain valley or cirque

KIOSK   A small information booth or structure

LOOP   Hiking out on one trail and returning on another

MASSIF   A large mass of connected mountains

MONADNOCK   Mountain that stands isolated or alone

OUT-AND-BACK   Hiking out and returning on the same trail

PRECIPICE   A steep cliff or rock formation

RAVINE   A steep, narrow gorge

SADDLE   A nearly flat low point between two mountains

SWITCHBACK   A trail that ascends or descends gradually back and forth

TARN   A mountain pond

TRAVERSE (n.)   A point-to-point one-way hike

TREE LINE   The location above which trees do not grow

appendix b: *outdoor shops*

CABELA'S
www.cabelas.com
475 East Hartford Boulevard, North
East Hartford, CT 06118
(860) 290-6200

CLIMB HIGH
www.climbhigh.com
191 Bank Street
Burlington, VT 05401
(802) 865-0900

2438 Shelburne Road
Shelburne, VT 05482
(802) 985-5055

EASTERN MOUNTAIN SPORTS
www.ems.com
2 Stephen King Drive, Suite 3
Augusta, ME 04330
(207) 623-2712

87 Marginal Way
Portland, ME 04101
(207) 541-1919

Fort Eddy Plaza
68 Ford Eddy Road
Concord, NH 03301
(603) 224-8781

Mall of New Hampshire
South Willow Street, Space W155
Manchester, NH 03103
(603) 647-0915

Main Street
North Conway, NH 03860
(603) 356-5433

100 Dorset Street
South Burlington, VT 05403
(802) 864-0473

INTERNATIONAL MOUNTAIN EQUIPMENT
www.ime-usa.com
2733 Main Street
North Conway, NH 03860
(603) 356-7013

LL BEAN
www.llbean.com
75 Evergreen Way
South Windsor, CT 06074
(860) 643-3840

95 Main Street
Freeport, ME 04033
(800) 559-0747

6 Wayside Road, Space T
Burlington, MA 01803
(781) 505-1460

appendix b: *outdoor shops*

LL BEAN

280 School Street
Mansfield, MA 02048
(508) 261-0400

8 Glen Road
West Lebanon, NH 03784
(603) 298-6975

REI

www.rei.com
71 Raymond Road
West Hartford, CT 06107
(860) 233-2211

401 Park Drive
Boston, MA 02215
(617) 236-0746

375 Cochituate Road
Framingham, MA 01701
(508) 270-6325

98 Derby Street, Suite 470
Hingham, MA 02043
(781) 740-9430

279 Salem Street
Reading, MA 01867
(781) 944-5103

22 Chapel View Boulevard
Cranston, RI 02920
(401) 275-5250

appendix c: *where to obtain maps*

APPALACHIAN MOUNTAIN CLUB
www.outdoors.org
(617) 523-0655

CLIMB HIGH
www.climbhigh.com
(See Appendix B for addresses and phone
numbers of stores)

DELORME
www.delorme.com
Two Delorme Drive
Yarmouth, ME 04096
(800) 561-5105

EASTERN MOUNTAIN SPORTS
www.ems.com
(See Appendix B for addresses and phone
numbers of stores)

INTERNATIONAL MOUNTAIN EQUIPMENT
www.ime-usa.com
(See Appendix B for address and phone
number of store)

LL BEAN
www.llbean.com
(See Appendix B for addresses and phone
numbers of stores)

MOUNTAIN WANDERER
www.mountainwanderer.com
Route 112
Lincoln, NH 03251
(800) 745-2707

REI
www.rei.com
(See Appendix B for addresses and phone
numbers of stores)

index

AMERICAN HIKING SOCIETY

Because you hike.

We're with you every step of the way

American Hiking Society gives voice to the more than 75 million Americans who hike and is the only national organization that promotes and protects foot trails, the natural areas that surround them and the hiking experience. Our work is inspiring and challenging, and is built on three pillars:

Volunteerism and Stewardship: We organize and coordinate nationally recognized programs – including Volunteer Vacations, National Trails Day® and the National Trails Fund –that help keep our trails open, safe and enjoyable.

Policy and Advocacy: We work with Congress and federal agencies to ensure funding for trails, the preservation of natural areas, and the protection of the hiking experience.

Outreach and Education: We expand and support the national constituency of hikers through outreach and education as well as partnerships with other recreation and conservation organizations.

Join us in our efforts. Become an American Hiking Society member today!

American Hiking Society

1422 Fenwick Lane · Silver Spring, MD 20910 · (301) 565-6704
www.AmericanHiking.org · info@AmericanHiking.org

DEAR CUSTOMERS AND FRIENDS,

SUPPORTING YOUR INTEREST IN OUTDOOR ADVENTURE, travel, and an active lifestyle is central to our operations, from the authors we choose to the locations we detail to the way we design our books. Menasha Ridge Press was incorporated in 1982 by a group of veteran outdoorsmen and professional outfitters. For 25 years now, we've specialized in creating books that benefit the outdoors enthusiast.

Almost immediately, Menasha Ridge Press earned a reputation for revolutionizing outdoors- and travel-guidebook publishing. For such activities as canoeing, kayaking, hiking, backpacking, and mountain biking, we established new standards of quality that transformed the whole genre, resulting in outdoor-recreation guides of great sophistication and solid content. Menasha Ridge continues to be outdoor publishing's greatest innovator.

The folks at Menasha Ridge Press are as at home on a white-water river or mountain trail as they are editing a manuscript. The books we build for you are the best they can be, because we're responding to your needs. Plus, we use and depend on them ourselves.

We look forward to seeing you on the river or the trail. If you'd like to contact us directly, join in at www.trekalong.com or visit us at www.menasharidge.com. We thank you for your interest in our books and the natural world around us all.

SAFE TRAVELS,

Bob Sehlinger

BOB SEHLINGER
PUBLISHER